SUPERNATURAL MARRIAGE

THE WAY IN

7 Proven Keys To Securing Supernatural Marriage

BY EVANGELIST VIVIEN ROSE

Published and Distributed
By Ignite Publishing House
E: ignitepublishinghouse@gmail.com
W: www.ignitepublishinghouse.com

IGNITE PUBLISHING HOUSE

A publication of
The Two Shall Be One
www.thetwoshallbeone.com

SUPERNATURAL MARRIAGE: **THE WAY IN**
7 Proven Keys To Securing Supernatural Marriage

CONTENTS

Supernatural Marriage: THE WAY IN

INTRODUCTION - What Is Supernatural Marriage?

STEP 1 – THE MORE EXCELLENT WAY

Laying The Right Foundation.

STEP 2 – THE ISSUE OF YOUR HEART

Positioning Yourself.

STEP 3 – HIS WIFE HAS MADE HERSELF READY

How God Prepares Women Versus How God Deals With Men.

STEP 4 – WHAT TO DO DURING THE WAIT

Plan, Possess, Occupy!

STEP 5 – SUDDENLY, IN A TWINKLING OF AN EYE

Supernatural Power and Speed

STEP 6 – BE FRUITFUL, MULTIPLY & HAVE DOMINION

Prosper, Fulfil Divine Purposes, Bring God Glory.

STEP 7 – GO SHOW OTHERS THE WAY

Now You've Attained – Go Propagate it!

WHAT IS SUPERNATURAL MARRIAGE?

Supernatural marriage is initiated by God for the peace, prosperity and propagation of healthy families and society. Supernatural Marriage is NOT like any ordinary marriage though marriage, per se is from God. Unfortunately, because of a lack of understanding of the purpose of marriage, many abuse the original intention marriage was designed. Supernatural marriage is are return to the Father's original intent for marriage. It is the highest gift of God to humanity after life and purpose. A precious gift released from heaven for the purposes of blessing man and glorifying God.

The beauty of supernatural marriage is a that it is God-orchestrated, God-connected and God-sustained union. The system of perpetual dating, and long engagements simply do not apply.

Anybody, single or married can prepare and position themselves in Christ to be a candidate for supernatural marriage. Singles prepare for it and married couples upgrade into it by choice. During this online course, you will learn THE WAY IN to receive the blessing of a godly marriage irrespective of your former challenges of delay, disappointment, divorce or marriage separation.

After 3 years of getting supernatural results in the ministry with hundreds of lives transformed to the glory of God, this signature course is highly recommended for Singles seeking a tried and tested way into supernatural marriage.

Why Does God Want Us To Pursue Supernatural Marriage?

For several reasons. First, supernatural marriage is His original foundation family and society.

God saw there was no companion for Adam, and He made that famous statement;

Genesis 2:18 *"And the Lord God said, "It is not good that man should be alone; I will make him a helper comparable to him."*

If we want peace, prosperity and dominion in the body of Christ, we must get back to doing things according to God's design in the beginning. We of all people should know the significance and importance of restoring divine orders in our families.

Genesis 2:24 *"For this reason, shall a man leave his father and mother and be joined to his wife and the two shall become one flesh."*

For what reason? For the reasoning of pursuing kingdom purpose, and for reason of walking in the blessing, prosperity, multiplication and dominion of Genesis 1:28. Ultimately for the reason of multiplying the godhead over the face of the earth.

Secondly, we should pursue Supernatural Marriage in order to safeguard lives from the perils of sexual immorality which is one of the biggest destroyer of relationships marriage and family. Sexual immorality is a cancer of soul and body, and it is an enemy of the welfare and health of our marriages, yet society is rife with it. Many sicknesses, diseases, mental health issues, abortions, premature deaths, youth delinquency, crimes and many other issues, can be traceable to somebody somewhere walking in sexual immorality.

So it is written, **1 Corinthians 7:2** *"Nevertheless, because of sexual immorality, let each man have his own wife, and let each woman have her own husband."*

This scripture right here points us to why God wants men and women, settled and married. It gives them responsibility, commitment, within an institution designed to eliminate promiscuity, sexual immorality and defilement. Basically, to avoid sexual immorality, God designed marriage for our benefit.

The bible goes as far saying, once a couple cannot exercise self-control sexually, let them marry. Instead of burning with passion, marry! Do you know how many men?

and women are sexually frustrated in our pews because of delayed marriage? Let us stop finding all kinds of new and inventive ways to satisfy ourselves sexually, and return back to monogamy, fidelity and love in marriage.!

1 **Corinthians 7:9** *"but if they cannot exercise self-control, let them **marry**. For it is better to **marry** than to **burn with passion**."*

These scriptures are written with an underlying assumption that all are able to marry or that marriage is easily available for those who wish to. Yet in this generation we are seeing an increasing number of single women IN CHURCH without any husband and many men, both in and outside of the church remain unmarried for decades. Something is wrong.

Does marriage guarantee fidelity? No. But does marriage encourage fidelity, yes.

Hebrews 13:4 *"Marriage is honourable among all, and the bed undefiled; but fornicators and adulterers God will judge."*

A third reason I believe God wants us to pursue Supernatural Marriage is, because it is His solution to restoring divine order in our homes, in His Church and in His Kingdom. Through Supernatural Marriage, God divinely planned a season of restoration of kingdom families. Now is that time. For years the enemy has been playing havoc with marriage and God is using supernatural marriage, to heal the pain of hope deferred in women. At the same time, He is restoring the hearts, the kingship and priesthood of men.

Last but not least, Supernatural Marriage is one the main platforms God is going to use to preach the gospel of the Kingdom and revive the nations in these end times. Through Supernatural Marriage, kingdom families will be empowered to fulfil the dominion mandate of Genesis

1:28 and attend to the Great Commission in Matthew 28:18-20. Righteous, godly marriage is the backbone of strong families and the success of every kingdom vision, ministry, business, outreaches and evangelism is dependent on us working together in families. In fact the Body of Christ cannot develop into her full maturity until her families are order.

Needless to say, supernatural marriage is a living witness of the Father's heart towards humanity. It will play a central role in preparing the Bride of Christ for His return even as the blessing it brings is enjoyed by thousands who felt denied, delayed or defrauded from their chances of being married, and raising a family which is a divine desire implanted deep in the soul of the majority of people. God is willing to fulfil that desire and has raised this ministry to assist His people into marriages that will fulfil them and glorify His Name.

Psalm 145:16 *"You open Your hand and satisfy the desire of every living thing"*

STEP 1 - THE MORE EXCELLENT WAY

Laying The Right Foundation

Key Scripture:

*1 Corinthians 12:31 "But earnestly desire the best gifts. **And yet I show you a more excellent way.**"*

Your story is a reflection of *His-story*. Every aspect of supernatural marriage is a picture or movie production of the *love-story* between Christ and His Bride - the Church. Supernatural Marriage is the story of the birth life burial, resurrection and return of Jesus Christ.

Every aspect of supernatural marriage is significant because it points to the love of God in Christ, towards us and the love of Christ for us through God. The imagery of marriage sets the scene for us to understand God is love. That is why marriage is traditionally viewed as a celebration of divine love.

The more excellent way teaches us about what true love is. When we understand God's kind of love, we are laying a great foundation to receive and sustain supernatural marriage.

1 Corinthians 13:1-10. "Though I speak with the tongues of men and of angels, but have not love, I have become sounding brass or a clanging cymbal. And though I have the gift of prophecy, and understand all mysteries and all knowledge, and though I have all faith, so that I could remove mountains, but have not love, I am nothing. And though I bestow all my goods to feed the poor, and though I give my body [a]to be burned, but have not love, it profits me nothing.

Love suffers long and is kind; love does not envy; love does not parade itself, is not puffed up; does not behave rudely, does not seek its own, is not provoked, [c]thinks no evil; does not rejoice in iniquity, but rejoices in the truth; 7 bears all things, believes all things, hopes all things, endures all things.

Love never fails. But whether there are prophecies, they will fail; whether there are tongues, they will cease; whether there is knowledge, it will vanish away. 9 For we know in part and we prophesy in part. 10 But when that which is perfect has come, then that which is in part will be done away.

Agape **Love** is the more excellent way. *Agape* is a Greek word meaning 'selfless love'. Others call it 'unconditional love' likened to the love of a parent towards a child. Agape Love denotes the "*the highest form of love, charity" and "the love of God for man and of man for God" – a pure, wilful, sacrificial love.*

This is how God loves. Selflessly, unconditionally, sacrificially, with pure motive. Allowing God to work on our character to emulate this in our relationships is the excellent way. Committing to doing things

His way, not our way is the green light the Lord looks for in a man and a woman to qualify them for supernatural marriage. He is always looking for people who will showcase His agape love to others, beginning with our most intimate relationships and then the world.

But you cannot give what you don't have. That is why the foundation of supernatural marriage is not looking for a husband or a wife, it is looking to Jesus who is the perfect lover of your soul. Building a love relationship with God through Jesus allows you to receive *Agape* Love and experience it for yourself. O taste and see that the Lord is good. When you receive this kind of loving, you become a different person. Your idea of love enlarges. Your capacity to love on that level increases and the more excellent way becomes your guide for relationships.

Seek to Know The Love of God for Yourself.

The first step on your journey towards supernatural marriage is, God will introduce you to Himself. Before praying for or pursing anything or anyone else, pray for yourself and ask God to show you His love. Experientially.

Ephesians 3:19 NLT *"May you experience the love of Christ, though it is too great to understand fully. Then you will be made complete with all the fullness of life and power that comes from God."*

Christianity is not so much about obeying a set a rules perfectly, though there are rules and commandments to follow. It is more about imperfect people building a love relationship with a perfect God so that our hearts are changed to become more like His.

Once you experience God's love, it will begin to overflow into other areas of your life. Committing yourself to the pursuit of the ***more excellent way***, in all areas of your life and relationships allows every other blessing attached to FLOW.

The More Excellent Way is Foolish at the Start and Glorious at the Finish.

Your example is Jesus who was born in a manger, raised in humble home, yet by His commitment to live by the ethics and standards of the 'more excellent way' He attained a position and a name above every other name.

At the beginning you may feel awkward. At times you will look foolish. But the more excellent way always delivers glory at the end. What does this have to do with supernatural marriage. Everything.

People rush into relationships, rush to be intimate, rush to showcase their victories and you may feel like you are taking the scenic route by 'waiting on God'. But your blessing of marriage is supernatural, meaning it is acquired with the approval seal of heaven. God the Father, God the Son and God the Holy Ghost giving you their full blessing and back up. Longevity, fulfilment and glory is what the Lord promises those who wait and do things His way.

Humility Is Not Stupidity.
Humility Leads To Glory.

In the Kingdom of God, the way up is down. Those who are willing to serve, sacrifice and wait on God's timings are exalted. Those who rush to compare and compete are eventually demoted. Listen to what the Lord taught us, then let us see His example: *Luke 14:11* NLT *"For those who exalt themselves will be humbled, and those who humble themselves will be exalted."*

Jesus practised what He preached and this is the mindset He wants us to develop. Longevity and happiness in marriage is attached to our ability to pursue the more excellent way. That is why money can't buy love, looks can't buy love, there is no price any person can pay for it. The price we pay for love to flow into our lives and marriages is not money, it is ministry – walking in agape love. That's the trigger for divine blessing.

The mindset behind the more excellent way is written in **Philippians 2:1-5** *"Let this MIND BE IN YOU. Esteem others, above yourself, Let nothing be done through selfish ambition or conceit but look out for your own interests and interest of others."*

Philippians 2:5-11 The more excellent way led Jesus Christ on a journey of submission surrender, obedience to the will of His Father in heaven and ultimately sacrifice which earned him a Name above every other name.

The Father elevates, blesses and opens the door of supernatural blessing to those who follow after the way of Christ.

A change of name and status is always attached to our willingness to pursue the more excellent way written in 1 Corinthians 13:1-10. For some that means promotion at work, for others, a higher anointing, for others breakthrough and for singles who are trusting God for a kingdom spouse, it paves the way for supernatural marriage.

Many follow His Word, their way but the Lord is looking for those who are willing to follow His Word, His Way. Not only will that bring you to the place of reward and blessing, it will position you to be elevated and bring God glory.

You can be assured of victory in Christ because GOD RAISED JESUS FROM THE DEAD it means when our obedience is complete God will also raise us up together with Him. In life He shall release and restore us into a position, a place and connect us with the person He designed for us to be with. God the Father takes no pleasure in withholding our marriages from us but He does want to PREPARE US this time around so that He can take pleasure in our marriages.

The more excellent way will safeguard us and deliver us from marriage dysfunction and breakdown. God's way works one hundred percent of the time. Through this simple step, the Lord will set you up for marital success, fulfilment and glory

STEP 2 – THE ISSUE OF YOUR HEART

Positioning Yourself.

Key Scripture:

Proverbs 4:23 *"Keep your heart with all diligence, For out of it spring the issues of life."*

So how you do position yourself for Supernatural Marriage? In short you become a facilitator not a frustrator of the Holy Spirit.

The Holy Spirit has an attribute like electricity. He is the livewire power of God in action. Electricity flows through lines and the wattage of the light bulb or power produced is a factor of the resistance created. Understanding this helps you to position your heart for the supernatural power flow of the Holy Spirit into your life.

The goal in positioning yourself for supernatural marriage is to remove as much resistance within you and around you to God's Spirit as possible. This is a journey which lasts a lifetime but the Lord will begin with you right where you are.

Positioning yourself starts with submitting our heart to transformation which is the epicentre of all spiritual, emotional and physical life.

So how do you become a facilitator of the Holy Spirit? Basically He works in us to remove what frustrates Him?

Philippians 2:13 NLT "For God is working in you, giving you the desire and the power to do what pleases him."

The Journey of Purification and Sanctification

Firstly from His name, we know He is holy so sanctification and consecration is a must.

"Be holy for I am holy" 1 Peter 1:16

This immediately calls for an end to all immoral relationships, friends with benefits and partnerships.

A right heart accepts this and asks the Lord for grace and strategy to EXIT or disconnect from any relationship which prohibits the free flow of the Holy Spirit into their life and atmosphere.

Secondly, it is written: *"Pursue peace with all men, and holiness without which no man shall see the Lord." **Hebrews 12:14***

This scripture gives us another clue about what frustrates the Holy Spirit and drives Him away. Strife and defilement. It says 'pursue' which means it is attained in measures over time; it is a lifelong pursuit in our journey of faith. Nevertheless Jesus said, *"if you love Me, obey my commandments" **John 14:15***; so God still expects us to maintain specific standards written in His word as we live out our lives for Him on earth. Obedience is key.

The Holy Spirit loves and moves over the Word of God to produce Christlikeness in our character. Galatians 5:22-23 lists for us the fruits of the Spirit which will manifest in our lives once we subject ourselves to His leading.

Galatians 5:22-23 *"But the fruit of the Spirit is love, joy, peace, longsuffering, kindness, goodness, faithfulness, gentleness, self-control. Against such there is no law."*

Ephesians 5:9 *"for the fruit of the Spirit is in all goodness, righteousness and truth."*

In scripture He is depicted like a dove which is gentle and sensitive (Luke 3:22, John 1:32, Matthew 3:16) and also as fire, as seen on the day of Pentecost. Acts 2:1-3.

We are instructed in *Ephesians 4:30* "*Do not grieve the Holy Spirit of God, by whom you were sealed for the day of redemption*"

The easiest way to summarize it, is having a clean heart, and maintaining a clean lifestyle, pleasing to God.

Therefore, being at peace in yourself and living at peace with those around you matters. If you are naturally contentious, or cantankerous, that is a sign of an unhealed heart. Men point the finger at women and women at men. Meanwhile the issue of hearts is a personal walk of transformation.

Positioning yourself begins in the heart. It is with your heart that you believe and have faith to receive the promises of God.

It is your heart of faith which will sustain you to continue and complete the process to attain the promise of supernatural marriage.

It is the heart where issues of relationships are birthed or aborted. Our ability to believe, love, obey, submit, trust depends on the state of our hearts.

Divine Qualification

Acts 10:34 *"Whoever believes and works righteousness is accepted by Him."*

The divine qualification to be a candidate for supernatural marriage is to believe in your heart, work righteousness and you will be accepted by God.

Positioning yourself in heart is having FAITH and believing for yourself.

Irrespective of your starting point, God will not use your history against you but through faith He gives you an opportunity to rewrite your history.

Through Faith you can escape your history and enter in destiny. Through faith you may have had a sad beginning and receive a happy ending. Hallelujah!

Hebrews 11:6 *"Without Faith it is not possible to please God. For all who come to God must BELIEVE HE IS and a rewarder of them who diligently seek Him."*

Look at those Jesus commended when He was on earth. He always commented and commended people when He saw faith in action. And He was always frustrated with people who had little faith. So faith is a big deal to God.

True Faith is expressed in action, in your speech, in decision and choices we make. True faith is not just heard, it is seen. There is evidence of it in your life

You can know a man or woman of faith by their actions not only by their words. James said show me your faith with no works. I will show you my faith by my works. Faith without works is dead. James 2:14-23

God told Abraham when he ACTED to obey Him to sacrifice Isaac – *"Now I know You Fear me since you have not withheld your son from Me."* - **Genesis 22:12**

Let us look at two women who had the wrong foundation but faith released them into supernatural marriage.

You may have been known for something immoral in your history. But it is not too late. If you will position yourself to give your heart to the Lord Jesus Christ and surrender your life to SERVE HIM alone, then He can include you too.

Story of Rahab - Joshua 2:1-18 in the natural her job, her line of business, her reputation disqualified her. A harlot and the woman who ran the business. She owned the whore house.

She was the madam of the Hareem for crying out loud. Yet in ONE DECISION TO DEFECT TO GOD she went from being disqualified to qualified.

Rahab stopped serving herself, serving mammon, (because it paid handsomely) and serving a system of sexual immorality and begun to serve the people of God and His kingdom She helped the spies who came to check out the landscape of Jericho.

Joshua 6: 24-25 *"they burned the city with fire and all that was in it with fire, only the silver and gold and vessels of bronze and iron they put in the treasury of the house of the Lord and **Joshua spared Rahab the harlot her father's household and all that she had. So, she dwells in Israel to this day because she hid the messengers whom Joshua sent to spy out.**"*

Hebrews 11:21 *"By faith Rahab did not perish with Jericho because she received the spies with peace."*

Many know Rahab was spared.

What many don't know is she is in the lineage of Christ through a supernatural marriage. She became chosen and was rewarded with a righteous husband. Common!

Rahab was the mother of BOAZ. Boaz was the supernatural husband of Ruth and Ruth was the mother of Jesse who became the Father of King David. All of them were part of the lineage of Christ and their names were written in Matthew 1:5-6.

How about that for a generational reward?!

Supernatural Marriage is a reward to those who please God by becoming facilitators of what He is doing not frustraters of His Kingdom agenda.

Story of Ruth - Ruth was also disqualified in the natural. She was a Moabitess and Moabites were descendants of Lot through incestuous relationship between Lot and his eldest daughter. They had become thorns in flesh for children of Israel and always troubled their peace. So, God troubled them and counted them as enemies of Israel.

Ruth was daughter in Law of Naomi who was widow to Elimelech who had died. Some years later, her two sons who both married Moabite women also died. Now it was against Jewish law for children if Israel from tribe of Judah to marry Gentile women, but RUTH MADE DECISION TO DEFECT TO GOD. She left her religion and her region and came out of her comfort zone to follow Naomi back to Bethlehem. She committed herself to Naomi and the God of Naomi when things didn't look promising.

Ruth 1:8 *"And Naomi said to her two daughters in law, Go return each to her mother's house. The LORD deal kindly with you as you have dealt with the dead a with me. The LORD grant that you may find rest each in the house of her husband"*

Oprah kissed her through tears and went back. ***But Ruth clung to her.*** The time comes when you must make a decision of NO RETURN.

No Return to your former life,

No Return to convenience

No Return to what you know, if it is wrong,

No Return to the Counterfeit Relationships

No Return to your former ways

The Supernatural Power flows when we make commitments of no return.

What will it be? Will you return like Orphah to the familiar, or cling like Ruth to faith and love?

Cling to the hope of God's promise even when things don't look promising. Working righteousness means taking risk on God.

He watches our choices.
He rewards our decisions.

Ruth 1:16 *"Entreat me not to leave you or to turn back from following after you for wherever you go, I will go, and wherever you lodge I will lodge Your people shall be my people and your God my God. Where you die, I will die and there I will be buried.* ***The Lord do so to me and more also if ANYTHING but death separate parts you and me."***

I believe when she made that vow to Naomi, God took it as her vow to Him and He rewarded her with a supernatural marriage to Boaz. That vow released Boaz. From that minute God ordered their steps back to Bethlehem and into to the field of Boaz who later put his eyes on her, and the rest is history!

Ruth positioned herself through faith enough to leave the familiar and love for Naomi and her God. It was enough to clinch her a supernatural connection.

Read the stories of other women come from the righteous side who received supernatural marriage:

- Rebecca Genesis 24
- Esther - Esther 2&5

Both of them positioned themselves in honour to God first.

What you have in your heart will express itself through what you do, whom you obey THEN what you have in your hand!!!

What About the Men?

Abraham is a man who believed for a supernatural promise of a son, despite the deadness his body and of his wife's womb, He did not waver at the promise through unbelief. He was fully persuaded that his promised son Isaac would be delivered, and it came to pass. (Romans 4:17-22).

Healing Your Heart

Jeremiah says it best *"the heart is deceitful above all things and desperately wicked, who can know it"*. **Jeremiah 17:** 9

Meanwhile one of the popular sayings of this generation is 'God knows my heart'. The word says; God looks on the heart or sees the heart but what does He see? He wants us to see, to acknowledge what is there in our hearts. That is the only way He can bring us to the point of conviction where we pray like David *"create in ME a clean heart and renew a right spirit within me"* **Psalm 51:10.**

Once David understood that his actions were attached to the corruption of His heart, He cried out to God. The corruption in his heart caused him to take another man's wife, sleep with her, impregnate her, attempt to hide it, then eventually to avoid the shame of being found out, he murdered her husband.

This is major! If we do not acknowledge the wickedness in our own heart in private it will eventually show up in public.

Look at the ugly progression in the life of King David; he went from lust, lack of self-control, covetousness, adultery, deceit and finally murder all manifested as a result of impure motives and thoughts in his heart.

Jesus taught "it is not what goes into the mouth that defiles a man but what comes out of the mouth, this defiles a man" Matthew 15:11 then He continued later;

Matthew 15:16-20: So, Jesus said *"Are you still without understanding? Do you not yet understand that whatever enters the mouth goes into the stomach and is eliminated? But those things which proceed out of the mouth come from the heart and they defile a man.*

For out of the heart proceed evil thoughts, murders, adulteries, fornications, thefts, false witness, blasphemies. These are the things which defile a man but to eat with unwashed man does not defile a man"

Saying 'God knows my heart' will *not* position you for supernatural marriage. David grabbed a woman and eventually married her BUT the bible says God was *displeased* with the method He used to gain her as his. He slept with her because he wanted her, plain and simple without

thinking about the consequences. He forgot about the will of God, the way of God and the word of God. He simply went for it because that was what He wanted, and He had the power and position to get it.

Ha! Where has the man after God's own heart gone? His heart had corrupted!

Sin corrupts your heart friends. It colours the lens through which we see right and wrong and makes us susceptible to self-deception first, believing we can get away with it. None of us are exempt from being vulnerable to sin. The book of James, says it this way;

James 1:13 *"Let no one say when he is tempted, "I am tempted by God'; for God cannot be tempted by evil, nor does He Himself tempt anyone. But each one is tempted when he is drawn away by his own desires and enticed. Then when desire has conceived, it gives birth to sin; and sin when it is full-grown, brings forth death."*

If not corrected sin will take you to a place where you no never thought you could go! Left unchecked, you may longer even care about the values and standards you once held dear. Before you know it, like David, you become a thief, a liar, a murderer and a deceiver or worse still a reprobate. Lord deliver us from ourselves! Seriously though, it is time for a reality check because

Many men and women live like this on a daily basis then convince themselves they are serving God. If you are reading this, there is still time to turn back! God is giving you a chance to escape and enter into newness of life and lifestyle.

This is why we always say, positioning and preparing yourself to receive the blessing of supernatural marriage is the same process through which you prepare yourself to be part of the 'Bride of Christ'.

Ask yourself, how many times have you justified your behaviour to yourself instead of permitting the word and the Holy Spirit to convict you and transform you?

We are all guilty of this at some stage. Nobody is exempt. It is pride which makes us point to everyone but ourselves. Pride is the major resistor to the flow of the Holy Spirt. It is written, *"...for God resists the proud, but gives grace to the humble"* **James 4:6, 1 Peter 5:5**

Grace includes God's mercy, unmerited favour, divine enablement, power, and help necessary to overcome temptation or be forgiven and restored when we fall into sin and repent of it. Grace also means the power God gives for believers to live free from a sin. Grace does not mean the license to cover up or excuse sin.

Therefore, saying to yourself *'God knows my heart'* will not help you to position yourself for supernatural marriage. Only a change of attitude from presumption to prayer will.

The correct approach is to prayerfully submit to God in prayer and ask Him

"Search me O God and know heart; See if there is any wicked way in me, and lead me in the way everlasting" **Psalm 139:23-24**

This process is worth the work because it is the same process through which your life will be prepared for the return of Christ. This prayer facilitates the Holy Spirit to get to work in you . He will remove impediments to intimacy with God and mould your heart into one where you can enjoy a healthy loving, long-lasting relationship with your husband or wife.

We all hear stories of people who are married yet no peace. Married yet not intimate. Married yet at loggerheads. Married yet unfaithful. Married yet unhappy. Why? The answer is the same, unhealed hearts and pride.

The hearts of those individuals need to be healed and drained of pride. Do you understand that No relationship can overcome the contamination of pride? Love stalls where pride is present. If God resists the proud because He cannot stomach it, what makes us believe we can sustain happy relationships when we are full of it.

As a single, even married couples, we strongly recommend you use your waiting season or separated season to take a good look at your heart. Before we go any further, I recommend do a heart check using the list below:

Purification & Sanctification - removing all forms of impediments and defilement in heart soul spirit. This is where sexual immorality, soul ties, shame insecurity, guilt, is broken. This is where soul wounds are healed. Be honest with yourself and with God. Hiding gives the enemy legal ground to keep you in bondage, fear or shame.

Psalm 62:8 *"Trust in Him at all times, you people; Pour out your heart before Him; God is a refuge for us. Selah*

Ephesians 5:11 *"And **have no fellowship** with the unfruitful works of darkness, but rather expose them*

Signs Of Unhealed Heart

Constant Worry, Anxiety

Fearful, Timid, Cowardly

Suspicious and Untrusting

Unfaithful, Disloyal

Easily Offended

Unforgiving, Unmerciful

Ungrateful, Complainer

Judgemental and overly critical

Religious, Self-Righteous

Unfeeling, Uncaring

Argumentative, Quarrelsome

Petty, Petulant

Controlling Spirit

Performance Driven

Perfectionist,

Jealous and Envious

Attention Seeker

Provocative Behaviour & Dressing

Low Self-worth and Esteem

Signs of Unhealed Heart (cont'd)

Boastful and Arrogant

Self-Admiration, Narcissistic

Prideful

Selfish, Self-seeking

Hateful, Hurtful

Vengeful, Betrayer

Mean Spirited

Social Climber

Position, Title Minded

Greed, Gluttony

Lack Self-Control

Short fuse, Angry, Violent,

Abusive, Malicious

Temperamental

Deceitful, Liar

Rebellious

Stubborn, Self-willed

Jumpy, Grumpy, Touchy

Aggressive *or* Non-Assertive

Overly Independent, Reject help

Another syndrome I refer to often is *'Mr Always Right and Mrs Never Wrong'*

By now I am sure there are several things on the list with which you identify with. Unless you are not human! Whether you struggle in one area or several areas, the state of your heart will not discount you unless you absolutely refuse to allow the Lord work on it. It is the power of God - the Holy Spirit – which works in us to will and act according to His good will. (Phil 2:13)

Create in Me A Clean Heart

What Signs Do You Identify With? (This is a journey, not a destination. Begin with honesty)

_____

_____

_____

_____

_____

_____

_____

_____

Lay Them Out Before The Lord And Ask God To Heal You, Purge Your Heart

_____

_____

_____

_____

_____

_____

_____

Document Your Progress

Month 1

_____

_____

_____

Month 2

_____

_____

_____

_____

Month 3

_____

_____

_____

Month 4

_____

_____

_____

Month 5

_____

_____

_____

Month 6

_____

_____

_____

Month 7

_____

_____

_____

Month 8

_____

_____

_____

Month 9

_____

_____

_____

Month 10

_____

_____

_____

Month 11

_____

_____

_____

Month 12

_____

_____

_____

Testimonies / Answered Prayers

_____

_____

_____

_____

_____

_____

Give God twelve months and you will not need to wait twelve months to see Him work!

God the Father does not expect us to work on it alone. Truth be told, it is near on impossible to change without help. All He asks for is surrender, co-operation and transparency in your relationship with Him. Things you cannot admit to others, you can acknowledge before Him and He will not reject, judge or condemn you. He will get to work on you and in you to produce godliness in character and nature.

Be mindful you may still need a trusted minister, person or counsellor to minister to you so you can be completely free. God will direct you in this.

The aim of this exercise is to transform you into a man or woman who is able to maintain

intimacy with God and also live peaceably and happily with others, beginning with your loved ones and supernatural spouse. Hallelujah!

The good news is, there is nothing broken in our hearts which heaven cannot heal. There is no wound deep enough where His loving grace cannot reach. The key to receiving healing for your broken heart, rejection, depression, hatred, shame or any other soul wound is *being willing* to be transparent to the Lord. No more excuse, no justifications, no more hiding.

You would be amazed how many people live in denial over the state of their heart. Like players on a football field, they block, they defend, they attack, anything and anyone who even attempts to correct them. Lord have mercy. I believe you want help, because you invested in this course and this workbook. So first off, will you make a decision to open up your heart to the Lord and allow Him to touch you in your inward man.

John 6:37 *"All that the Father gives Me will come Me, and the one who comes to Me I will by no means cast out"*

Jesus said this to give you confidence to COME! He will not reject you, no matter how bad you feel your heart is. Come. Ask Him for a new heart today.

God the Father will begin work right away to 'create in you a clean heart and renew a right spirit within you' Psalm 51:10. There is a connection between the state of our heart and the contamination in our spirits. Let the Creator fix it.

Why Does Healing Your Heart Matter?

Healing your heart is a priority, even a precursor to preparing for supernatural marriage because:

1.   It is your heart which conceives faith for God's promises before you can birth the promise.

2.   Without a healed heart, (clean heart), many people abort the process. They are either unable to nurture the promise full time, and miscarry through unbelief, doubt, wavering, or sin OR they start relationships but don't have the tenacity to finish. This is often the root cause of rotational dating, and cycles of broken marriages and divorce. Any the time the going gets tough, they bail.

3.   Thirdly, a clean heart sets the atmosphere in which your relationships live and breathe. The state of your heart affects the quality of your relationship with God and with others.

In summary, positioning yourself for supernatural marriage is primarily a heart issue. You can start off from any place, as long as you are willing to have faith in God, believe in His promises, and work righteousness.

Secondly allow the Lord to heal your heart, so that you can sustain faith full term and build intimacy with Him so that He can prepare you to receive your husband or wife in a spirit of meekness

STEP 3 – HIS WIFE HAS MADE HERSELF READY

How God Prepares Women Versus
How God Deals With Men.

Key Scripture:

Revelation 19:7-8 *"Let us be glad and rejoice and give Him Glory for the marriage of the Lamb has come and* <u>*His wife*</u> *has made herself ready and to her it was granted to be arrayed in fine linen clean and bright, for the fine linen is the righteous acts of the saints."*

Before we even get into this, notice the above scripture says *'His wife'* has made herself ready. The wife is referring to the Bride of Christ, made up of men and women, youth and children, *males and females* who have lived before Him in faithfulness on earth, awaiting and expecting His return.

Remember supernatural marriage on earth is a foreshadow of the supernatural marriage between the Lamb of God, our Bridegroom King Jesus and His Bride, the Church. Therefore, men need to learn to see themselves as a 'bride' to Christ and prepare for the wedding just as much as women do. As a man on earth you are preparing to be a groom but, in the spirit, you are preparing to be the 'wife' of Jesus Christ. Hallelujah!

Secondly notice the intentionality of the above scripture. The wife made herself ready. No bride or groom gets married accidentally. The minute you know you are getting married; preparations and planning begin.

You Make Yourself Ready!

Supernatural Marriage is an intentional work of positioning, planning and preparation.

Supernatural Marriage is not accidental it is intentional.

Preparing for Supernatural Marriage As A Woman

Remember the bridal gown cited in Revelation 19:8 is the righteous acts of saints.

As a woman there are 10 keyways to prepare;

1. **Purifying your heart** (build your faith through regular hearing of the word of God and seek healing for your heart. The job of the five fold in the faith is to edify you, teach you the word, and minister to your needs but it is your job to make good on

what God has made available to you by building yourself up on your most holy faith.

Jude 20 (Maintain your life with God) *"But you beloved, building yourselves up on your most holy faith, praying in the Holy Spirit, keep yourselves in the love of God, looking for the mercy of our Lord Jesus Christ unto eternal life."*

2.   **Purifying your motives for marriage** – your devotion to Christ as your bridegroom King and husband will become stronger than your desire for a husband or a wife once the Lord begins to work on your heart.

3.   **Prayer and intercession** – women birth the plans of God into manifestation through intercession and prayer. Women have been given wombs to conceive, carry to term and deliver children. The same applies in our relationship with the Lord, Women are natural intercessors, called to conceive the divine seed of the Word of God, and to carry visions, assignments and destinies through to birth in prayer.

Prayer & Intercession Guidelines

Areas of Focus in Prayer

1. For yourself – relief yourself of fear and doubt and refuel your faith.
2. For your foundations of faith, love and honour to be restored
3. For restoration of godly men to be harvested into the kingdom
4. For divine alignment (as a man or woman)
5. For divine connection and discernment for the One
6. Pray against counterfeits and trap of 'Ishmaels'
7. Pray for speedy fulfilment of the promise

What is God Saying To You?

_____

_____

_____

_____

_____

_____

What Area Do You Sense The Lord Is Working On?

_____

_____

_____

_____

What are Your Greatest Fears? Share Them With The Lord

_____

_____

_____

_____

Who Do You Need To Let Go / Release / Forgive?

_____

_____

_____

_____

_____

Purpose: (Ask the Lord to Reveal His Purpose Your Life)

_____

_____

_____

Your Spouse (Write details the Lord reveals about your future husband / wife as you pray).

_____

_____

_____

_____

_____

_____

Document Prophetic Words Over Your Marriage

_____

_____

_____

_____

_____

Thanksgiving (Count Your Blessings, and Name Them One By One)

_____

_____

_____

_____

_____

Testimonies of Answered Prayers

_____

_____

_____

_____

_____

_____

_____

4.   **Intentionally SERVE** others. This habit prepares you for married life, which is ministry-of-helps all by itself. Service stops you being self-focused and self-centred. Note Rebekah was in service when Abraham's servant found her. She was quick to volunteer her service to water the camels in Genesis 24. Service is an attitude, as much as it is an act. Ruth was gleaning in the field to help make ends meet and take care of her aging mother-in-law Naomi. Those who serve well at one level are usually the ones promoted to the next level.

5.   **Sacrifice -** it was a sacrifice for Rahab to turn her back on her main source of income. Equally it was a sacrifice for Esther to leave behind her way of life. It was a sacrifice for Rebekah to water the camels. the act of seeding, sowing fasting or performing something at great cost to yourself in faith towards God. Sacrifice is what

Christ did on the cross to release the power of regeneration to reconcile man to God eternally by a single act of faith in Him. Sacrifice is what Solomon offered to God,

before, and after building the temple which provoked God to ask Him to name whatever it is, He wanted.

That is when He asked for wisdom and the LORD added onto him riches, long life and honour. Sacrifice produces lifetime rewards. Anytime you see sacrifice in the bible, you see God responding by releasing a lifetime reward.

Supernatural marriage is a lifetime reward and a generational blessing. So, sacrifice is one of the keys which opens the door and ushers you in. Rebecca in Genesis 24:15 sacrificed and this she was chosen to be the wife to one of the most eligible bachelors of her day, Isaac, who was the sole heir of Abraham. Rahab used the key of sacrifice by giving up her lucrative career of harlotry in Jericho, defecting to God by choice and faith, helping the spies from Israel and providing the people of God access into their promised land. It was her act of bravery and sacrifice the Lord rewarded. Esther became queen because of her sacrifice, not just in the three days fasting, but in leaving behind her family, dedicating herself to honour those in the hareem, and later interceding for her people. Her final war cry when she risked her life by breaking palace protocol and going before the king "if I perish, I perish". That single act of sacrifice ignites his love for her again, gave her an opportunity to plead deliverance for her nation and won her a name in the hall of faith. Her husband the

king offered her up to half the kingdom as her reward. This is the power of sacrifice. It touches the heart of God and releases the hand of God to work supernaturally in your life

Your seeds, sowing and sacrifice shall never be in vain when directed to the Lord in sacrifice

6. **Contend Together** – the resistance the devil has built up against marriage, especially godly marriages demands we contend together, for our inheritance of supernatural marriage.

Many singles grow weary, some have given up due to their attempting to journey alone. The wisdom of the daughters of Zelophehad in Numbers 27 is they formed a united plea for their inheritance and God released it to them. We fight together, we win together. We fight alone, we win or fall alone. It is that simple.

7. **Be Productive** and become fruitful in seeking the kingdom of God. What are you going to be named for? Every woman who received a supernatural husband in the bible was productive. Rebekah, Esther, Ruth and Rahab are such women. Every man who received a supernatural connection or breakthrough was equally productive. David was serving his Father's sheep before being promoted to serve in the palace before King Saul. Zacharia was serving in the temple. Joseph despite his predicament in prison managed the prisoners and ministered to the inmates.

8. **Apply Diligence** – is a special quality that delights the heart of God who releases supernatural rewards into your life as a result. Diligence is an elevator. Diligence is rewarded by God and admired by men. Ruth was commended to Boaz by her diligence in Ruth chapter 2. When he made enquiries about her, the report of her diligence stood out. Same with Rebecca. She was diligent to volunteer to draw water for Abraham's servant and for his camels. **Hebrews 11:6** says *"God is a rewarder of those who diligently seek Him"*

Diligence brings you before 'kings' – **Proverbs 22:29** *KJV*
*"Seest thou a man diligent in his business? **he shall stand before kings**; he shall not stand before mean men."*

9. **Fasting** – All is not lost if you are struggling to break through in marriage. Jesus has given us a way out. *"This kind can come out by nothing but fasting and prayer"* **Mark 19:29**

Fasting and Prayer

Esther is the physical picture of what God does in our spirit when we participate in the process of Fasting and Prayer.

Fasting changes YOU it doesn't change God. Fasting, builds our spirit, gives God an opportunity to work in us. Fasting helps us to break free from addictions of the flesh like soul ties, greed, gluttony, alcohol, and lust.

WHEN YOU PRAY, WHEN YOU FAST.

God expects us to pray and to fast. We see this by the statements Jesus made when He taught on the Sermon the Mount in Matthew Chapter six.

And <u>when you pray</u>, you shall not be like the hypocrites.......

But you, <u>when you pray</u>, go into your room, and when you have shut the door, pray to your Father who is in the secret place; and you Father who sees in secret will reward you openly. And <u>when you pray,</u> do not use vain repetitions as the heathen do. For they think they will be heard for their many words – **Matthew 6:5-7**

Jesus spoke this phrase **'when you pray'** three times in three verses Similarly, when He taught on fasting in the same chapter Jesus assumed it would take place.

<u>Moreover, when you fast</u>, do not be like the hypocrites, with a sad countenance...... But you when you fast, anoint your head and wash your face, so that you do not appear to be fasting, but to your Father who is in the secret place; and your Father who sees in secret will reward you openly – **Matthew 6:16-18**

There is no if or but about it, praying and fasting is part and parcel of walking victoriously with God in the Spirit. In fact, there are certain issues which we were warned by the Lord can come out ONLY by prayer and fasting,

So, He said to them,

"This kind can come out by nothing but prayer and fasting." – **Mark 9:29**

Benefits of Fasting

- Fasting helps us to heal and restore brokenness of spirit, soul and body. Many sicknesses and diseases are healed on a fast.

Isaiah 58:8 *"Then your light shall break forth like the morning, your healing shall spring forth speedily, and your righteousness shall go before you; the glory of the LORD shall be your rear guard."*

- Fasting supercharges our spirit and helps us renew our faith Especially when we get weary. That extra oil of intimacy with God will sustain you and give you endurance to stand until the end.

Isaiah 40:31 *"They that wait upon the Lord shall renew their strength, they shall rise up with wings as eagles, they shall run and not grow weary, they shall walk and not faint"*

- Fasting breaks bonds of wickedness, spiritual oppression, generational curses and iniquity.

Isaiah 58: 6 *"Is this not the fast that I have chosen: To loose the bonds of wickedness, To undo the heavy burdens, To let the oppressed go free, And that you break every yoke"*

Whatever has bound you will be broken through periods of fasting.

- Fasting accelerates us into our destiny because of the flow of God's power. Remember when we become a 'facilitator' of the Holy Spirit into our lives, His power flows.

I have never heard of anyone feasted their way into supernatural life. Including supernatural marriage. The power of the supernatural life of God flows through sacrifice, faith, unity and consistent prayer. The way of the world and the works of the flesh must be put to death.

We've talked about this in our positioning and preparing section. How God puts to death, crucifies the flesh. He works **in women** and works **on men** to mortify the flesh because FLESH is the enemy of supernatural marriage.

Dying to self is the system we discussed earlier in 'Step 1' The More Excellent Way.

Another overlooked blessing of fasting, is when you are on a fast, you are overshadowed with the presence of a sweet spirit, the aroma of virtue, godliness, faith, boldness and kindness.

When I began reading about Jewish weddings, one of the things which stood out to me was, both the bride and groom enter into their wedding day, fasting. The wedding vows and other rites are performed before the Bride and Groom eat privately afterwards. This is symbolic to me because fasting means 'denying yourself'. **Denial of self is the way to break the stubborn strongholds of marriage delay and denial.**

Delay is bond of wickedness. Delay seeks to frustrate the promises of God in our lives. Through the Lord uses delay in our single season, even permits it for a time, God never intends for delay to be denial.

10. **Dedication** – Hannah used the key of dedication to release supernatural promise from God. Whatever or whoever you dedicate to God, belongs to Him and shall be used for His purposes. When we dedicate our lives to Him, we give Jesus the license to rule and reign in our lives. When we dedicate our children as Hannah did in her prayer of dedication, we effectively give the Lord rights to intervene in their lives and become His for eternity.

Likewise, when we dedicate our marriages to the Lord in faith, it secures them for His glory and accelerates their release.

In all our supernatural marriage courses, we take holy communion and dedicate our marriages to the Lord. It is a vow of dedication, not to be taken lightly. It is a promise to not only be married but to be mindful to allow the purposes and glory of God to take pre-eminence in your marriage.

Making A Vow of Dedication Over Your Marriage to Honour The Purposes of God – 1 Samuel 1:10-12

Write it here:

_____

_____

_____

Outward Beauty versus Inner Beauty

Rebecca was beautiful and a virgin too...but that's not everything! Virginity and beauty was just a basepoint; that's not what makes you unique!

Esther was also beautiful and a virgin, yet this was not the basis upon which she was chosen to be queen. Supernatural marriage does not depend on the absence of competition, it depends the presence of favour.

The story of Abigail who intervened and stopped David from killing her husband Nathan and all that they had, was also described as beautiful.

A few days later, she was released from her marriage as God took her wicked husband. The minute King David heard of it, He sent her a marriage proposal which she readily accepted. The Lord resettled her in the palace, married to the King, albeit it not the only wife, as an honour of her sacrifice.

Ladies beauty is to be admired; beauty attracts the man but favour secures Him as your husband. No one acquired a supernatural marriage by being beautiful and a virgin. ALONE. The world will make you believe, beauty rules.

Well not in heaven honey!

Outward beauty is great and making yourself look good matters but inner beauty trumps them all because of the favour it brings

Proverbs 31:30 – *Charm is deceitful and beauty is passing, but a woman who fears the Lord, she will be praised."*

How Do Men Position and Prepare Themselves for Supernatural Marriage?

The foundation is the same, lay the right foundation with the more excellent way, prayer and dealing with issues of the heart. However, one aspect the Lord revealed to me is, the heart of men is different to that of women. God has fashioned the heart of a man separately to the heart of a woman; therefore, he deals with us accordingly.

With men, the Lord focusses on outwards circumstances to tutor, prepare and refine them for marriage. God our Creator works on men and women in different ways. **He works in women and on men** when it comes to creating in us a clean heart. Knowing our makeup and sensitivities, the Father is a master at draining pride out of our hearts, but the process varies.

Through this process, He crucifies men in flesh and circumcises their heart.

In essence, God prepares men to be able take up the mantle of Ephesians 5:22-33 teaching them *the way of* Christ to become the 'saviour' of the body (their family) through sacrificial love, and servant leadership. Most men are NOT TAUGHT THIS. The position of headship is emphasized to them without clear directives on the responsibility that comes with it. Every position of leadership has a job description, and being a husband is no different. It is a spiritual office of leadership, appointed by God for men to carry out specific duties in His name and for His purposes. God fathers men so they can emulate Him and father their wife, children and household. The way of Christ with His Bride should reflect on the way of every godly man and His bride.

Currently in the church, there is greater emphasis on women being ministered to concerning how to be a godly wife than there is on mentoring men to become godly husbands. Men are left to their own devices to decide how to operate and this needs to change. Scripture doesn't
simply state men are the head of their wives, it instructs them HOW they are to carry out that duty. By allowing Christ to be their head. They are to follow His lead. When we see it like that, half of what men call leadership or headship is error.

In the Body of Christ, if we are to end the dysfunction in our marriages, we must become just as intentional in preparing our sons, and men to become husbands as we are on preparing our daughters to become wives. Many men did not have a good example in the home, but God is a good good Father. Through the revelation of the way of Christ, men can re-establish godly leadership again in their homes and bloodlines.

Remember as a man, the bridegroom it is possible for you to also be delayed! Throughout the lifespan of this ministry I have noticed certain patterns.

1. Men with great callings upon their life, anointed men, godly men with pure hearts have experienced delay. I have come to understand through prayer and seeking the mind of God, this is because they need women of a certain calibre, that meet a set criteria to be their wives. These women are simultaneously being prepared by God to handle the anointing upon their lives.

2. Another common scenario is women who have been called to intercede for men who are still in the world yet carry a great destiny. These faithful women in Christ are assigned these men by the Lord and their kingdom assignment is to carry and cover their assigned man into the safety of their destiny through intercession. It is a process of submission, love and humility like no other. This is exactly

what Miriam did to Moses, when He was a baby. She ran alongside the bank, looking and checking on him until he was safely delivered into the palace. These assignments are not easy and require great grace because often nothing seems to be happening. However, the Father favours these women greatly.

Intercession is the greatest labour of love next to martyrdom. When you intercede for someone, for their soul, salvation, deliverance, welfare, that they may fulfil destiny, you are acting in the very nature of Christ Jesus Himself. **John 15:13** *"Greater love has no one than this, than to lay down one's life for his friends"* To the Father you are not only praying for a supernatural marriage, you are laying down your life.

3.   Other men are delayed due to being in a wrong relationship. They are living out of divine alignment. When the Lord gave me the charge to lead this ministry, He made it clear, that many wrong relationships would break down, in order for right to take place. Especially non-covenanted relationships, but not exclusively. Some wrong relationships include marriages that were put together by man, human choice yet were never the counsel of God to begin with. Unfortunately, this is a painful reality

God knows, there are certain relationships He redeems with the willingness of the individuals involved. For others despite many prayers, fasting, and every known counsel known to mankind, God still permits the marriage to fold. I have heard countless testimonies of men and women who are honest enough to confess in the midst of their devastation, the Lord revealed to them, He had released them from their marriage because their ex-wife or ex-husband was not in alignment with His will for their life, nor His purposes. Others suffered untold abuse and to safeguard their destiny, the Lord sovereignly saves them out of the sinking ship of a rotten marriage. That was my personal testimony.

The word clearly says 'He whom God has put together, let not man separate" –

Matthew 19:5 *"For this reason a man shall leave his father and mother and be joined to his wife, and the two shall become one flesh'? **So then, they are no longer two but one flesh. Therefore, what God has joined together, let not man separate."***

It is sin for any third party to interfere in a marital relationship, and equally it is a sin for the married couple themselves to cause divorce in a marriage brought together by God. That is why divorce must be repented of regardless of whose fault it is. Whether you chose carnally or your marriage crashed or whether you aborted a marriage union given birth to by God; repentance, forgiveness and a return to God's ways is the only antidote for healing and restoration.

It is not a slight thing in the sight of God to treat marriage disrespectfully and trivially. It is a major transgression of His will and word. However, like all sin, we serve a God of a second chance who desires for us to get it right the next time – hence why He has commissioned this book and e-course "Supernatural Marriage - The Way In".

We pray your testimony will become one of the stories which will bring God glory as people see the power of Jesus Christ in redeeming you out of the pit of brokenness, divorce, abuse, carnality, addiction, perversion, adultery or whatever affliction caused your former relationship to break down.

I speak in more depth about this in the message, currently on our YouTube channel **"5 places your husband is going to come from"** You can listen to it here: https://youtu.be/UstfJTfURdA (YouTube Channel: The Two Shall Be One)

Out of these 5 places, the shortfall of eligible godly men in the church will be replenished.

- The prodigal man
- The carnal man
- The unbelieving man
- The younger man
- The Jewish man.

The Lord explained to me the reasons behind each type of man so it's worth a listen.

How will God Raise & Release Husbands?

As we pray for men, the Lord revealed some time back that He is **'recreating the heart of husbands again'** in men, according to the righteous standards laid out in scripture. He used the story of Jeremiah 18:1-4 to speak to me. Just like the potter could remake another vessel which became marred in his hands, so is God the potter in our generation, remoulding hearts and lives of men into another vessel, as seems right to Him.

Jeremiah 18:3-6 "*So I went down to the potter's house, and I saw him working at the wheel. **But the pot he was shaping from the clay was marred in his hands; so the potter formed it into another pot, shaping it as seemed best to him**"*

*Then the word of the LORD came to me. He said, "Can I not do with you, Israel, as this potter does?" declares the LORD. **"Like clay in the hand of the potter, so are you in my hand, Israel.***

Secondly the Lord is removing the filthy garments from the His sons in the kingdom and bestowing upon them rich robes and a clean turban. So, they can serve Him in their spiritual office without defilement.

Zechariah 3:1-5 "Then he showed me Joshua the high priest standing before the angel of the LORD, and Satan standing at his right side to accuse him. The LORD said to Satan, "The LORD rebuke you, Satan! The LORD, who has chosen Jerusalem, rebuke you! Is not this man a burning stick snatched from the fire?"

Now Joshua was dressed in filthy clothes as he stood before the angel. The angel said to those who were standing before him, "Take off his filthy clothes."

Then he said to Joshua, "See, I have taken away your sin, and I will put fine garments on you."

Then I said, "Put a clean turban on his head." *So, they put a clean turban on his head and clothed him, while the angel of the LORD stood by."*

Hallelujah! These scriptures should give you hope. What we are about to see in these end times is a global harvest of the souls of men into the kingdom, serving Christ as kings and priests unto God. (Revelation 1:4-6).

Right now there seems to be a famine or deficit. I decree in this generation there shall be a turnaround and godly men shall overflow in our churches again. Not church goers, Christ lovers. Men after God's own heart. Men with the Father's heart, willing to seek His agenda. Truly there is no problem on earth which God cannot solve. He is the Almighty, El Shaddai, able to do exceedingly, abundantly above all we can ask or think.

Once you catch this revelation you are motivated to rise up to deal with the problem. We are able to overcome it, together! Rehashing the problem won't get us far. Faith is what is required, backed up by willingness to give ourselves consistently to the work of intercession, fasting, sacrifice, mentoring, and evangelising of men. Our Bridegroom King is coming soon, and His sons will not be missing. The deficit will be restored. Praise the Lord.

So how does the LORD prepare and position men for supernatural marriage?

He crucifies their flesh.

Yes, you heard right. He crucifies the flesh and circumcises their heart. When the Lord revealed this to me, it all made sense. What the Father did to His firstborn Son, Jesus in gaining a wife, surely, He must do to all other sons seeking a supernatural bride. Ha! Jesus is the Way.

So, God puts men through a process of difficulties, challenges, frustrations and even permits them to face opposition, affliction and devastation in order to teach them the obedience, and submission to His word as godly husbands in the making. I heard one man say, God gave him the 'gift of pain' before he was ready to do marriage God's way.

God knows the heart of men, so He tailor creates a series of issues, challenges for each man, which includes season of opposition like Isaac in digging the wells, years of service and financial injustice like Jacob or sacrifice and delayed answers to prayer like Abraham and Joseph

For how long? Until they surrender.

10 Ways God Deals With Men

Women worry about the state of the men. Not understanding that the Father breaks them down before building them back up. You think nothing is going on, until you see the finished product.

THE FATHER KNOWS what men need even before they do.

Genesis 2:18 *"And the Lord God said It is not good that man should be alone; I will make him a helper comparable to him".*

1. **He Puts Men to Sleep Like Adam** until their 'Eve' is ready or mutes them like Zacharias so that they do not mess up the process. Genesis 2:21-23 and Luke 1:13-20

2. **He Isolates Men Like David**. IN order to draw himself, God isolates him from people. These men often face rejection not realising it is a redirection to give the Lord opportunity to build up greater intimacy in private before being elevated publicly. The Lord reserves them for a set time. Meanwhile He works into them a spirit of humility, and faithfulness in service.

David is a typical example of this.

I Samuel 16:1 God sent Samuel to Jesse his Father's house.

1 Samuel 16:6-10 Jesse parades His sons.

1 Samuel 16:11-14 they called for David who was isolated from his family.

God may anoint you for an office or assignment but keeps you hidden for a time because he knows, he knows the sharks; "sauls" are looking to kill them. Out of jealousy, envy and insecurity. Davids are reserved to replace those in office who fail God.

3. **He Devastates Men** like Jonah, Apostle Paul and King Nebuchadnezzar who were all devastated by God. Men of means, men in ministry who rebel or walk in high levels of pride are setting themselves up for divine devastation. God orchestrates situations to swallow that man's ego pride and rebellion so that he submits and surrenders.

- Jonah was devastated in the belly of great fish 1:4
- Apostle Paul was devastated on road to Damascus. Acts 9:11-7
- King Nebuchadnezzar was devastated by being driven to live like an animal for 7 years to bring him to his senses. By Daniel chapter 4, he had learned his lesson and begun to bless the God of Daniel 4:36-38

4. **He Drives Men Into The Wilderness Or Exile** like Moses and Jesus. This process kills selfish ambition, self-motivated works, self-righteousness works and teaches them obedience to follow God's timing.

- **Exodus 2:11-22**. Story of how Moses went into exile

- **Luke 2:41-52** Jesus already had command of the scriptures by age twelve, but He went back into obscurity and submitted Himself to His parents until it was His time to for ministry, aged thirty.

- **Luke 4:1-2** The bible says immediately Jesus was baptised in water at the beginning of His ministry, He was driven by the Holy Spirit into the wilderness to be tempted of the devil.

So, process has to be followed.
You must still fulfil all righteousness until your set time.

5. **Men Serve Under Godly Leadership, Mentors or Fathers** like Joshua, Elisha and Prophet Samuel. The apostles also served three years under Jesus.

- **Joshua** served under Moses (Numbers 11:28)

- **Prophet Samuel** served under Eli the Priest. (1 Samuel 3:1)

- **Elijah raised** Elisha (1 Kings 19:19-21)

- **Jesus raised by godly father** (Matthews 13:55)

- **Jesus raised 12 apostles** - (Matthew 10:1-4, Mark 3:13).

6. **God Reveals His Glory to Men** as in the days of Isaiah. In revealing His glory, the men see themselves, their shortfall and need of His grace.

- **Prophet Isaiah** sees the glory of the Lord (Isaiah 6:1-7)

- **Apostle Peter** sees the glory of the Lord (Luke 5:1-8).

7. **God Wrestles With Men Through Injustice** as He did with Jacob and Joseph. He wrestles with their will until they are no longer self-willed or feel entitled, self-righteous or vengeful. Through the process of handling injustice, God works in them, humility, wisdom and compassion. He gives them an understanding, generous and forgiving heart.

- **Story of Jacob** – Genesis 32:22-32

- **Story of Joseph** – Genesis chapter 37-41

8. **God Imprisons Men** for a season in a place or by a problem in order to protect their lives and callings. To train them, teach them discipline, give them time alone, develop them into manhood

- **Joseph was put in prison, until Genesis 41:1** when Pharaoh had a dream that Joseph was released from prison. (Psalm 105:19 confirms, the word of the :God tested him until it was time)

- **Saul converted to Paul in prison** (Acts 9:1-7) Isn't it ironic, that the same man who used to imprison others, now becomes a prisoner of Christ himself. (Acts 8:3)

Note: when men are imprisoned because of the work of the devil God releases them supernaturally through prayer. When there is a divine purpose in it, the Lord works with them until it is time.

- **Acts 12 Herod put Peter in Prison** and God delivered Him.
- **Acts 16 Paul and Silas prayer** and praised and foundations of prison were shaken.

9. **God Permits Men to Face Battles & Challenges to Teach Them to War.**

David in wilderness overcame the paw bear and the lion before killing Goliath.

He wrote **Psalm 144: 1** *"Praise the Lord, who is my rock. He trains my hands for war and gives my fingers skill for battle."*

Psalm 18:32-37 *"It is God who arms me with strength and makes my way perfect. He makes my feet like the feet of deer and sets me on my high places. He teaches my hands to make war, so that my arms can bend a bow of bronze."*

When they took the promised land, it says that God intentionally left some of their enemies in the land, so that he could test the children of Israel and train them to fight

Judges 3:1-2 *"Now these are the nations which the LORD left, that He might test Israel by them, that is, all who had not known any of the wars in Canaan (this was only so that the generations of the children of Israel might be taught to know war, at least those who had not formerly known it"*

10. **God Wins Them And Woos Them By His Goodness And Love:** Scripture says, it is the goodness of God which draws men unto repentance. When God woos men, He calls them and gives them an assignment. Jesus did this when He called His disciples. Mark 3:13, Matthew 10:1-4

You will know a man is being wooed by The Lord because they are transformed through a having and personal love relationship with

Jesus. The apostles had such an intimate walk with Jesus over three years that their love bond kept them strong through persecution, martyrdom into eternity. Even though Apostle Paul was not present, He built up a similar love bond with Christ. To the point where he said, "to live is Christ, to die is gain" (That is the language of a man smitten by divine love.

This tenth point includes calling men back from the dead - spiritual, physical, and emotional death. I believe the power behind resurrection is love. God's love is so strong, that it can pull those He loves out the grave. He did to His own Son Jesus and Jesus did it many others including Lazarus when He was alive. Agape love resurrects! In the story of Lazarus (John 12:38-44), I see the command of Jesus to Lazarus to come forth as the demand God is making on the world right now to give up His Sons! *"Lazarus Come Forth!"*

The main divine motive behind everything God is doing is to bring men to REPENTANCE because we are reaching the fullness of time. Some of his methods may seem harsh in the present but for a good end. The heart of our heavenly Father is to redeem restore and rescue any man who will learn from the process so that he can inherit the promise.

Romans 2:4 *"Or do you despise the riches of His goodness, forbearance, and longsuffering, not knowing that the goodness of God leads you to repentance?"*

- His Chastisement tutors' men to repentance.

- His rebuke steers men away from error.

- Hi Spirit convicts men of sin, righteousness and judgement.

- His hands bind the wounded up and His love woos them and wins them back to Himself.

- If need be, He resurrects them.

Some men stubbornly continue down a long road of rejection, rebellion, devastation or recluse before coming to their senses. Our prayer for every man reading this book, is you will turn back, sooner, rather than later. Everything God does or has permitted into our life is used to bring us into a repentant mindset. Not only for us be sorry or remorseful but *He wants for us to admit we have gotten things wrong by doing things our way.* Somehow the painful realisation of failure and trouble prepares our heart to freely choose to *do things His way. Selah.*

STEP 4 – WHAT TO DO DURING THE WAIT

Plan, Work, Occupy!

Key Scripture:

Matthew 25:1-13 The Parable of the Wise and Foolish Virgins

"Then the kingdom of heaven shall be likened to ten virgins who took their lamps and went out to meet the bridegroom. Now five of them were wise, and five were foolish. Those who were foolish took their lamps and took no oil with them, but the wise took oil in their vessels with their lamps. But while the bridegroom was delayed, they all slumbered and slept.

"And at midnight a cry was heard: 'Behold, the bridegroom [a]is coming; go out to meet him!' Then all those virgins arose and trimmed their lamps. And the foolish said to the wise, 'Give us some of your oil, for our lamps are going out.' But the wise answered, saying, 'No, lest there should not be enough for us and you; but go rather to those who sell, and buy for yourselves.' And while they went to buy, the bridegroom came, and those who were ready went in with him to the wedding; and the door was shut.

"Afterward the other virgins came also, saying, 'Lord, Lord, open to us!' But he answered and said, 'Assuredly, I say to you, I do not know you.'

"Watch therefore, for you know neither the day nor the hour [b]in which the Son of Man is coming."

Store Extra Oil

During the Wait

Waiting for a supernatural marriage is not easy. It may take years, as I am sure you have discovered. The blessing of this season is God is looking to release singles into marriage supernaturally and fulfil His promises NOW. We live in a time when the promises He gave His sons and daughters are now being fulfilled. The process of positioning, preparing, planning and being released into Supernatural Marriage does not need to be longer than twelve months. That is the truth!

For those who have waited for years, this seems unlikely. But it is true, nonetheless. In years past, the Father spoke prophetically concerning His plans towards those who desire to get married. For many, there seemed to be a delay which has brought a sense of frustration or dejection. Thousands of women remain single who have waited years for the manifestation of what the Father spoke to them over ten, even twenty years ago.

I am happy to announce, the season has changed from waiting to manifestation and fulfilment. What the Lord spoke in times past is now happening, in greater numbers around the world and the prophesied avalanche of divine connections, supernatural weddings, marriages and reconciliations is at the doors. We must update our minds concerning this else the enemy will make you believe; it is for a later season. Remember every promise has a timeline. There is a deadline to this, because these marriages hold an eternal purpose to usher in revival and the glory of God.

Ecclesiastes 3:1 & 8 *"To everything there is a season, a time for every purpose under heaven....... (vs 8)..a time to love and a time to hate..."*

On the timeline of heaven, it is now the season and more importantly the TIME (Kairos moment) for an avalanche of supernatural marriages to be released globally! Praise God. Be encouraged, you are positioned and preparing for this to happen to you, at the right time in history.

However, be warned, as you prepare and wait in expectancy for your ordained spouse, you must be diligent to avoid what the bible calls foolish virgin syndrome. What is that?

Having no reserves.

What Is Your Contingency Plan?

When you plan on a long journey, a car trip or vacation, wouldn't you take refreshments and supplies? Of course! You would check there is enough fuel and food for the journey and pack "extra" in case. Especially if you a parent.

The wise go a step further, they check out the services available along the way because they want to ensure, in case of any delay, they are covered.

This is the same mindset you have to carry when waiting for supernatural marriage. The promise is your destination. The journey is always longer than expected, delays should be planned for even though the manifestation is sudden, unexpected and speedy.

The parable of the five wise and five foolish states categorically the difference between the two groups was *extra oil*.

This stage of the wait can be likened to the so-called delay of the return of Christ. Scripture says many will scoff in the last days, saying, nothing has changed, he is not coming. Many will grow tired during the wait because they made no contingency plans to keep their faith buoyant, active and alive during the wait.

2 Peter 3:3-4 *"knowing this first: that scoffers will come in the last days, walking according to their own lusts, 4 and saying, "Where is the promise of His coming? For since the fathers fell asleep, all things continue as they were from the beginning of creation."*

Likewise, many men and women waiting for the promise of supernatural marriage, have not made any contingency plan to sustain their faith during the wait. That's where weariness

comes in, doubt creeps in, temptation, frustration and if you don't apprehend yourself, the enemy will pressure you to give up on the journey all together.

Same way people are saying "Where is the promise of His coming?" is what they say concerning supernatural marriage. "Where is it, when is it?" As sure as I am that one day Jesus will return, I know *in my knower*, the avalanche of supernatural marriages shall also come. Oh yes!

So, as a 'wise virgin' believer, you must make plans to stay on track. What are you feeding you soul? How are you boosting your faith? Who are you connecting with to encourage you? Do you have enough spiritual supplies for the journey? The faith food you eat today doesn't prevent you from getting hungry tomorrow.

Only the five wise virgins who carried extra oil entered into supernatural marriage. In Matthew 25:1-8, there were ten virgins who waited, ten virgins prayed for a husband (of wife as it may be), ten virgins weary and slept but when the bridegroom came, only five virgins were ready to go in! For lack of extra oil, the window of opportunity was shut when the five foolish virgins frantically went to go and buy extra oil.

Remember this applies to men and women because the virgins were all waiting on ONE groom who is Jesus. So, men and women must be virgin-in-spirit-and-heart, betrothed to Christ, keeping themselves for Him alone, not dipping and diving in and out of relationships, dating, playing with the world or soiling their garments. The wise were busy storing extra oil.

The five wise virgins (made up of faithful men and women) did not depend on their natural capabilities alone to get married, they

depended on the grace and favour released from the presence of God. They trusted in His timings and kept themselves pure and unspotted from

the world. (James 1:27). The five virgins were people who made contingency plans to boost their faith walk so that even at their weakest moment, they would not buckle.

One thing which alarms me about this parable is that, despite their good intentions, only 50% of them inherited supernatural marriage when the Groom came. Ouch!

Why Did the Foolish Virgins Not Carry Extra Oil?

I believe it is because the extra oil costs. The worst part of this story is the price is not beyond what any sincere person can pay. But there is a price, nonetheless. Remember in this parable, the five had to go 'buy it' (Matthew 25:10) and in that time, the door to supernatural marriage was shut. The season was over. Which means the oil costs. The oil is TIME invested in building intimacy with God, time invested in prayer, and fasting; time spent in the Word, time spent pursuing purpose, time invested in serving God, time invested in learning, time spent sowing, sacrificing, serving….you name it. The extra oil can only be built up over time.

The word is clear, God rewards our faith.

Hebrews 11:6 *"Without faith, it is not possible to please God. For he who comes to God must believe, He is, and He is a rewarder to them who diligently seek Him."*

We know 'faith without works is dead." (James 1:17) So how much time we spend in actively seeking the Kingdom of God personally and through our various endeavours for the Lord is accounted to us as 'faith works.'

When Jesus instructed us in *Matthew 6:33*; *"Seek first the Kingdom of God and it's righteousness and all other things will be added to you"* He knew this was a protection and buffer from weariness. **Keeping yourself active, busy for God eases the wait**. Becoming fruitful, pursuing vision, building, working, occupying new territory for God keeps you focussed. It also keeps you out of trouble friends!

God is a rewarder of them who diligently seek Him. Not conveniently seek Him. Diligence is a characteristic which carries us into the promise of supernatural marriage. Extra oil is not a hit and miss affair.

Just as the earth produces oil from coal and minerals being consistently pressurised under the earth's surface, so is your extra oil produced under pressure.

No wonder the Lord permits a season of delay, no wonder He permits a season of waiting, working, warring, worshipping and wearying. Those who press through the pressure are building up their oil reserves!

This extra oil is the one which produces Christ like nature, so when the Bridegroom comes, we will be like Him. **Jesus does not want to be unequally yoked to His Bride, any more than we want to be unequally yoked with our supernatural husband or wife** on the earth.

That means there is seasoning of suffering in the flesh yet becoming alive and mature in spirit.

Listen please my friend, every child of God has a measure of faith and anointing but it takes personal investment to carry extra oil. That's the demarcation God made between the five wise virgins who were 'ready' and the foolish virgins who waited alongside them but were actually not prepared.

Can you see how tight this thing gets? Supernatural Marriage is available to all but how many truly desire to position, prepare and plan for it?

Let me say it once more; in preparing yourself for supernatural marriage, make contingency plans to store up extra oil.

Actively Work on Yourself and Kingdom Assignments

In reference to supernatural marriage, there are certain the LORD works on both couples simultaneously. He works to bring men, the bridegroom, into alignment with His will and He works on helping women, the bride, to make herself ready.

God waits for the Bride to have prepared herself, with her gown, her righteous acts, her extra oil all be in place. As well as storing extra oil, use your single season to work on yourself, beautify, exercise and get busy working on the projects and dreams in your heart.

This is in keeping with the command of Jesus for us to occupy till He comes.

Luke 19:13 KJV *"And he called his ten servants, and delivered them ten pounds, and said unto them, Occupy till I come"*

The New King James Version says it this way *'do business until I come'.*

Your waiting season is not the time to slow down, slack off or watch the clock. Your waiting season is an opportunity for you to pursue, possess, build, occupy!

Before you get married, challenge yourself to become bigger, better, bolder in pursuit of your kingdom purpose and dreams. Do business, travel, write, research, invest, live life to the full and use your talents in the services of God.

In a word, be **productive**. There are so many examples in the bible of this. Both men and women. Before they experienced supernatural breakthrough or marriage, they were found in the place of **productivity and service.**

- Joseph was **productive in prison.** (Gen 39:21-23)
- David was **tending His father's sheep** in the wilderness, fighting off bears and lions. (1 Sam 16:11,

1 Sam 17:34-36)

- Ruth was productive, **gleaning in the field**, before marrying Boaz. (Ruth 2:2-3)

- Rebekah **serving the needs** of her family before marriage to Isaac. Genesis 24:16-22)

- Esther was productive, **beauty preparations and learning palace protocol** before marrying the King (Esther 2:9-15)

- Zacharias was **actively serving in ministry** in the temple of the Lord before his elderly wife Elizabeth supernaturally got pregnant. (Luke 1:8-17).

Productivity Check

What Are You Doing with Your Time?

_____

_____

_____

What Are You Currently Producing or Working On?

_____

_____

_____

Where or How Are You Serving Others?

_____

_____

_____

_____

What is in Your Hand / What is in Your House / Identify
Your Gifts

_____

_____

_____

_____

_____

_____

**If there is nothing, concrete, you can point to, ask the Lord
to put you to work!**

Supernatural husbands and wives are people of purpose.
Actively engaged in kingdom business of some kind. You
could at home like Jael in Judges 4:17-18 or on the war front
like Deborah and Barak. The issue is, you should actively
seek to be productive in the Kingdom of God. The Lord

releases assignments on a daily basis, there is no excuse not be employed by heaven.

When a widow of the Prophets who had died came to Elisha with her late husband's debt she was distraught. He asked her, what do you have in the house.

She said, nothing but a little oil in the house. That 'little oil' became a business and supernatural source of income which cancelled her debts. Do not underestimate yourself or what you carry.

[Read the full story] **2 Kings 4:1-7**

Idleness towards the things of God is a thief of your time and opportunities.

Women when your husband comes, you won't have a long time to prepare to be a wife. Suddenly you have to switch into wife mode. That is why the Lord is emphasizing maximise your season of preparation with planning!

Begin walking in the area of your purpose, assignment now. Single Ladies, by experience, I have discovered the women who are 'found' walking in their field when their husband is connected to them, find it easier to develop in it, once they get married than the married women do, who discover or attempt to launch out after they've been married for a while. Especially women in ministry! Why? Because the woman is the centre of the home so anything she does SHIFTS and the equilibrium of the home feels destabilised. Some men like the status quo and feel threatened by any change, so their first reaction, if they are insecure is to try and get you to rethink it, shelve it a little longer or worse still, some block it all together.

Unfair, maybe so. It is life for many women. Not all men assist their wives at first. Listen, even Joseph, (Matthew 1:19-20) who was a just man in the bible, wanted to put Mary away. What greater assignment on earth can a woman be entrusted with, than to carry, birth and raise the Messiah? Jesus the anointed One! Thankfully the Lord intervened through a divine dream visitation.

But that shows you, men, even with the best of hearts can misconstrue what the Lord has called you to do and put up a resistance at first. Prayer towards this end is important. Pray the Lord will reveal His counsel to your husband or future husband. Nevertheless, practically speaking; women it is wiser and easier for you as a Single woman to be FOUND already walking in the field of your endeavour. Your husband accepts you as He finds you.

The same goes for you as a man. I personally know men whose wives frustrated their lives, the minute they discovered they were called into ministry. I know of women who left their husbands because they dared to obey the call of God upon their lives. There are women who do not want to sacrifice to help their husbands build. Truth! They simply want to enjoy the fruits of what he has already built. So to avoid this costly mistake, BEGIN NOW. It cuts down the risks and chances of connecting to a counterfeit woman or man for marriage.

If you want to lose weight, do it now. Buy your wedding dress now. Grooms get some money set aside for when your bride is presented to you. When it comes to attire, I highly recommend going for fittings, shopping for your venues, clothing, makeup, hair styles as soon as possible. As a guideline, we always recommend, you want to be in the position that *if you needed to get married within 3 months*, it is possible. I am not saying you have to, I simply mean, prepare yourself to the point where you are in a position to move quickly!

Start that business now. Launch out into ministry now. Write that book now. Get your finances in order now. Do whatever it takes, in the midst of the pressure of the wait to pursue your purpose during your single season. This is the best way to prepare and plan towards supernatural marriage. Not by waiting and whining. By waiting, planning and working. Being fruitful and faithful unto your first love, Christ Jesus.

STEP 5 – IN A TWINKLING OF AN EYE

Supernatural Power and Speed

Key Scripture:

1 Corinthians 15:22 *"in a moment, in the twinkling of an eye, at the last trumpet. For the trumpet will sound, and the dead will be raised incorruptible, and we shall be changed."*

1 Thessalonians 4:17 *"Then we who are alive and remain shall be caught up together with them in the clouds to meet the Lord in the air. And thus, we shall always be with the Lord."*

God will always present wives to their husbands. Just like He did for Eve in Genesis 2:22 when God presented Eve to Adam, the Lord will usher the women as brides into the lives of the men He has designated for them to marry. It's not up to you to look for your Adam. God will introduce you to your Adam. God is interested in your receiving the gift of supernatural marriage.

Men know their wives by the spirit. God has put the knower

in men and the discerner in women. Adam instinctively knew this woman carried his DNA, carried his substance, carried something in himself. That is why many times men seem to be able to engage so quickly and know early on who they want to marry. God has gifted me with the capacity to look beyond the outward beauty and see something of themselves in you – their wife. That is their missing rib.

No woman has to convince a man to marry her. Men know ladies and they know early. Ask men from different walks of life, men in Christ, or regular men in the world, 99.9% of them will have similar testimonies. Within the first few meetings,

of meeting their wife, they made up their minds, she was the one for them.

It is the knower God gave Adam in Genesis 2:22-24. Most men know the woman they wish to pursue into marriage. Many don't tell her right away because they feel it's too early for her to accept them. But they know.

Note: Until a man gets to the place he desires marriage,

nothing can really move him. He must want it. That is where the prayer comes in for men to mature and grow up into manhood. Many are afraid to commit. Afraid to take on responsibility of marriage. Afraid of getting hurt again so fear plays on men's minds a lot. We bind that spirit in the mighty name of Jesus!

So, there are exceptions to this rule is when the man himself has issues with marriage, or there is distance which may bring procrastination. Nevertheless, even in this circumstance, intercession will work better than coercion.

Work with the Lord, stand your ground, maintain a lifestyle of sanctification, know your worth and trust God to do the inner work necessary to help that man understand you are a 'wife' not a 'girlfriend'.

The price your Father in heaven has put on your life, as a daughter in Christ, is covenant. He doesn't stop at commitment. God demands covenant. The commitment of a man is known when he is ready to covenant with you in marriage. Nothing less is accepted.

Final warning to men and women concerning sex I need to say this. Men, when you feel entitled to conduct an intimate relationship *outside of a marriage* covenant; to the Lord, it is fraudulent. To God it is theft.

See what it says in;

1 Thessalonians 4:4-8 *For this is the will of God, your sanctification: that you should abstain from sexual immorality; that each of you should know how to possess his own vessel in sanctification and honour, not in passion of lust, like the Gentiles who do not know God;* **that no one should take advantage of and defraud his brother in this matter, because the Lord is the avenger of all such,** *as we also forewarned you and testified. For God did not call us to uncleanness, but in holiness. Therefore he who rejects this does not reject man, but God, who[a] has also given us His Holy Spirit.*

Likewise, sisters, when we willingly use our bodies to seduce and prey on the weakness of men for our own pleasure or gain, for whatever purpose, outside of marriage covenant, once again it is viewed as a fraudulent transaction by God and theft.

Hebrews 13:4 *"Marriage is honourable among all, and the bed undefiled;* ***but fornicators and adulterers God will judge.***

So, when we considering entering into a relationship with someone, let us be mindful of the sin of seduction, and be put our cards on the table. What do you want with her? Where do you see this going? What do you want with him? If marriage is not on your mind, let them go! That's only fair. Someone else will value them as a life partner.

Secondly remember what we said earlier, women receive divine favour before marriage and men receive divine favour after they step into marriage. **Proverbs 18:22** *"When a man finds a wife, he finds a good thing, and receives favour from the Lord"*

Because Supernatural marriage is God initiated. He is the Father who, gives away His daughter into the hands of His son.

The church, the bride of Christ will be brought into the presence of Jesus our bridegroom during the rapture. The twinkling of an eye speaks of the speed at which we go from being betrothed, to being married. **The avalanche release of supernatural marriages is a prophetic picture of the Rapture.**

- God presented Eve to Adam – Genesis 2:22

- God presented Rachel to Jacob – Genesis 29:9-28

- God even permitted Leah to be presented to Jacob Genesis 29:18-21

- God presented Rebekah to Isaac – Genesis 24:66-67

- God presented Esther was presented to King Ahasuerus – Esther 2:17

- God presented Ruth was to Boaz – Ruth 2:5, and Ruth chapter 3

- God represented Mary to Joseph – Matthew 1:20-24.

- God will present The Church, The Bride of Christ to Jesus (at the Rapture)

Ladies, God will present you to your husband. He will divinely connect you, present you either in person, online or even in a dream to your husband. Somehow, someway he will make the divine connection. He will lead you, guide you, instruct you like Ruth, put you in his eye view for long enough until he turns his head. Then he opens His heart. Bam! Love begins to flow.

We have had ladies, whose husbands saw them and received dream confirmation that this was their wife. I have heard this happen more than once.

One gentleman told us how the Lord taught him to choose purpose over outward preference. Having been disappointed with his former decisions, this time he fasted. The Lord revealed his wife's heart in a dream. They met at a wedding of a mutual friend.

Though they got on, it was not until the Lord confirmed that she was 'the one' with the beautiful heart, that he moved into action. Within weeks he proposed, and they married within months. Praise God, they have been happily married now for over 10 years with three children.

Time will not permit me to share all the stories we hear. But rest assured, when you are walking in divine purpose or area of gifting, you are one hundred percent guaranteed to meet your husband when you **live in alignment with God for your life, pursuing your kingdom purpose**. That's the fastest way for the Lord to connect your paths. God will do the connecting, you focus on the praying, positioning, preparing and planning.

Supernatural marriage is the HIGHEST gift of God on earth, aside from salvation!

It's not a matter of if, it's a matter of when. It will happen. Hold fast to your confidence. Don't be swayed by what you see or feel or what's happening around you. It will happen by the power of the Holy Spirit.

Luke 1:45 *"Blessed is she (or he)* **who believed***, for there will be a fulfilment of those things which were told her from the Lord."*

One of the first signs of supernatural marriage is the Groom comes ready, because
the Lord works on men in a different way to women. We talk about this in detail in '10 Ways God Deals with Men' in earlier chapter.

Once that long awaited, day dawns and the divine connection with your ordained husband or wife is made; we have seen most couples only wait a 3-6-month window to organise themselves before they are married. It is that quick!

There have been testimonies where people spent a year but usually this is due to external influences which hinder the couple or even demonic attacks which worked to frustrate the marriage union being confirmed and consummated.

A Sign of The End Times

Supernatural marriage is a prophetic image, sign of the end of times. Jesus alluded to this when He said in **Matthew 24:37** *"But as the days of Noah were, so also will the coming of the Son of Man be."*

He was making reference to **Genesis 7:9** *"two by two they went into the ark to Noah, male and female, as God had commanded Noah."*

God brought the animals together and they went in two by two, forming a long 'train' or 'trail' into the ark. Likewise, God is bringing couples together 'male and female' two by two to win souls into His ark. **Your supernatural marriage will be part of a global parade of couples, a glorious 'train' signifying the bridal train of the Bride of Christ.** Through these marriages, the Bride of Christ will carry souls into the ark of eternity. Hallelujah!

Be expectant for your supernatural release.

In a Twinkling of an eye, it shall come to pass.

If Jesus, our soon coming Bridegroom King is not lying about his return to take His Bride to heaven, He wants you to know, neither is He lying about connecting you to your kingdom mate; your supernatural husband and virtuous wife. He has it scheduled as part of a bigger plan. Amen.

There is a role we play in activating marriage miracles and there is a role the Holy Spirit plays in releasing marriage miracles.

I have a nickname for the Holy Spirit when it comes to marriage, He becomes *"The Propellant"* He is the fuel and the fire. When we light the match through activations below, holy combustion takes place!

Activating Marriage Miracles

The Miracle in Your Mouth

ACTIVATION 1 - THANKSGIVING

Thanksgiving is Heaven's Transformation Room

One of the keys to activating the miracle of multiplication is being thankful and blessing God with the little we have. What men and women have been doing for centuries is complaining against each other and the situation in our relationships has only worsened.

Jesus used this activation key to feed the five thousand, by multiplying five loaves and two fish. When we bless the Lord by thanking Him for the little good, He turns little into much. I learned this on the Singles Tour in America. The Father said to me, what the nations needs is more godly men. So, on Thanksgiving Night, in Texas, He asked us to 'bless Him and thank

Him for all the good men and godly men standing in the nation'. He would receive our thanksgiving and activate the process of multiplying and transforming godly men back into the nation. This key will work in any community, any nation where there is a felt lack of eligible men to marry.

When we show our gratitude for the few; heaven goes to work to multiply more of the same back into our lives and communities. **Listen my dear friends, we have a role to play in replenishing the kingdom with more of what we desire – kingdom marriages.** As a woman thank the Lord for every godly husband, as a man thank the Lord for every virtuous wife.

For those who are married, be grateful for the good in your partner. Bless the Lord for the good that remains. Heaven will go to work on the rest. With our words and a change of heart, we can transform our world! Starting Today. **Be Thankful with Your Little.**

Matthew 14: 16-21 *"But Jesus said to them, "They do not need to go away. You give them something to eat."*

And they said to Him, "We have here only five loaves and two fish."

*He said, "Bring them here to Me." Then He commanded the multitudes to sit down on the grass. **And He took the five loaves and the two fish, and looking up to heaven, He blessed and broke and gave the loaves to the disciples;** and the disciples gave to the multitudes. So, they all ate and were filled, and they took up twelve baskets full of the fragments that remained. Now those who had eaten were about five thousand men, besides women and children.*

The Amplified Bible says Jesus *'gave thanks'*.

The Kingdom key of miraculous multiplication is giving thanks with our little and offering it to God. He sees our gratitude multiples it.

Even Now Pause to Give Thanks for Every Kingdom Marriage?

In every area, you wish to see multiplication you can begin to activate your miracle through the act of sincere thanksgiving. What Do You Lack? What Do You Seek? Before asking for more, give thanks to the Father in heaven for what you have. Lift it up before God in appreciation. Celebrate with those who are walking in the very blessing you desire, and God will multiply that same grace back to you.

ACTIVATION 2 - PROPHESY!

The story in Ezekiel 37 and the dry bones used the activation of prophesy. Speaking and decreeing into existence the word of the Lord, the will of God and commanding the winds of the earth, and the Ruach (wind of God's spirit) to move things and people into position. Prophesy to the bone-of-your-bone to connect to you! Prophesy to that the Spirit of God will divinely locate and connect you to your husband or wife. Prophesy LIFE back into the fabric of your marriage. Prophesy!

Read Ezekiel 37:1-11 for the whole story.

This is how it starts;

Ezekiel 37:3-4 *"And He said to me, "Son of man, can these bones live?"*
So, I answered, "O Lord God, You know."

Again He said to me, "Prophesy to these bones, and say to them, 'O dry bones, hear the word of the Lord! ⁵ *Thus says the Lord God to these bones: "Surely I will cause breath to enter into you, and you shall live.*

Now it is your turn. PROPHESY!

_____

_____

_____

_____

ACTIVATION 3 - PRAISE

There is always a supernatural response to our praise. On a personal level the Word of God says the Lord is "enthroned in the praises of His people…" inhabits the praises of His people". (Psalm 22:3) When we praise the Presence of God manifests because He comes down Himself to receive it from our lips. At the same time, your praise elevates you to where God is. High and lifted up, far above the issue. Reigning over it in Majesty. Praise reduces the problem in our own eyes and enlarges God in the midst of the situation.

Corporate praise in the days of King Jehoshaphat confused the enemy. The praise team went out ahead of the army and they didn't need to fight. Their praise activated God to fight for them. All those who had ganged up against Judah were defeated. Praise the Lord!

2 Chronicles 2:21-22 *"And when he had consulted with the people, he appointed those who should sing to the Lord, and who should praise the beauty of holiness, as they went out before the army and were saying:*

"Praise the Lord,
For His mercy endures forever."

Now when they began to sing and to praise, the Lord set ambushes against the people of Ammon, Moab, and Mount Seir, who had come against Judah; and they were defeated"

Corporate praise also released the power of God to bring down the wall of Jericho before Joshua and the children of Israel. O God in heaven, let every barrier and wall of resistance to our kingdom marriages crumble before our praise! Amen.

Joshua 6:20 *"So the people shouted when the priests blew the trumpets. And it happened when the people heard the sound of the trumpet, and the people shouted with a great shout, that the wall fell down flat. Then the people went up into the city, every man straight before him, and they took the city."*

Don't take these activations lightly. One of my closest friends in ministry was divinely connected to her husband 3 days after the Lord asked her to offer Him up a sacrifice of praise. With a. dance!

ACTIVATION 4 - UNITY

Unity is a major key to the release of supernatural power. It is unavoidable if we want to see the power of God working in our lives. As I study those who walk in supernatural power and during my travels on the mission field, there are two keys I have discovered which set the right conditions for miracles:

First we must strive to be in union with God, full of faith, godly character and the Spirit of God. (Acts 6:2-7)

Secondly always seek to pray in unity with like-minded believers trusting God for the **same thing**. Focus on one subject at a time. Scattered focus in prayer is not as effective as honing in on one area. This is crucial. God's power is like a laser beam, it flows towards a given target. Being in one accord, in one place, seeking ONE thing always release power! (Acts 2:1-4, Acts 4:23-31)

Jesus said where two agree concerning a matter, the Father will do it. He was talking about heart to heart agreement.

Matthew 18:19 *"Again I say to you that if two of you agree on earth concerning anything that they ask, it will be done for them by My Father in heaven."*

This is where association really counts. Disconnect from the naysayers, the negative crowd, unbelieving crowd and mocking crowd. Connect with people of faith who believe in the supernatural power of God. Too many Christians are religious in their outlook, debating the whys and wherefores of supernatural marriage. Meanwhile the examples are littered throughout the Bible. Don't worry about arguing with people, connect with those who believe. You are trusting God to receive your divine inheritance. Don't allow people to waste your time with many debates.

Psalm 133:1 *"Behold, how good and how pleasant it is for brethren to dwell together in unity"*

ACTIVATION 5 - MOVE WHEN HE SPEAKS

Moving when the Holy Spirit is flowing is key to supernatural breakthrough. Mary, the mother of Jesus told the servants at the wedding, "Whatever He tells you to do, do it". Simple instruction that released supernatural power Before manifestation there is always an instruction. Be committed to TOTAL obedience. Whatever God is leading you to do may seem unrelated now but the miraculous is ignited when we move when He speaks. Remain sensitive to the promptings of the Holy Spirit and respond. Fast!

"Be quick in your response time to the promptings of the Lord. Embedded within His instructions are breakthroughs and miracles. The Lord gave me insight into the fact that

most people who received a breakthrough, a miracle, a blessing from Him while Jesus walked on the earth did so because they seized the opportunity as He was working, walking, waiting or moving. Wow!

When the Spirit is God is moving in an area, we must learn how to jump into the flow of what He is doing rather than be totally disconnected yet expect the Lord to attend to our request. Your needs and desires will be met as you avail yourself to be part of what He is doing in the earth.

Stop being so set in your ways. It is GOD who knows what is good for you and what you WANT. Be willing to act in faith in UNPLANNED TIMES. Don't always expect Him to move during a set event or program only.

- The Woman with the Issue of Blood in Matthew 5:22 moved and was healed.

- Zacchaeus climbed a tree to see Jesus passing by and salvation came to his house. (Luke 19:4)

- Blind Bartimaeus heard Jesus was passing by and cried out! All the more. He saw opportunity in the midst of opposition. He took a chance where others saw his disadvantage. (Luke 18:39)

- The Four Friends who carried their paralytic friend on the mat. broke through roof to let him down in front of Jesus. (Mark 2:4)

Move when He speaks is the fifth activation that will help you receive a miracle from the hands of Jesus. As Nike would say, Just Do It!

Activating Marriage Miracles

The Propellant (Holy Spirit)

Effortless Love Connection

How is it possible for a man to love a woman, like Isaac did to Rebekah yet He didn't even know her for a long period of time? How is it possible for a woman like Esther to find grace and favour in the sight of a gentile King so much so, that He put the royal crown upon her head? How is it possible that the heart of Jonathan, King Saul's son was knitted to the heart of David upon hearing his voice? How is it possible for you to believe that men know their wives, many on first meeting, others within a few meetings. How does this supernatural marriage thing work?

It is only possible by the **FAVOUR OF GOD**

The effortless love connection that marks supernatural marriage is a mystery until we understand divine favour and voice activation The same Holy Spirit who sheds abroad the love of God in the heart of a believer, is the same Holy Spirit who opens the heart of a man to love his wife on sight. It is the same Holy Spirit which connects the hearts of women to their husbands. The same Holy Spirit who favoured Mary, and by His Power, overshadowed her to become pregnant is the same Holy Spirit who releases Singles into marriage.

You see the secret ingredient to supernatural marriage is WHO turns on the switch of love in our hearts towards one another when we meet. God is love and so when He favours a person or a relationship, He releases His grace (favour) over those same

people and love begins to flow. It is still received by choice because we choose to move with the love we sense or we block it. Love is a gift, you either receive it or reject it. It is love nonetheless.

The effortless love connection is another hallmark of supernatural marriage. Through all the stories cited, except for Leah, love was present from the very beginning. It doesn't make sense until you understand it is a divine activation of the Holy Spirit imparting His love into our hearts.

Voice activation – is another secret ingredient to supernatural connections and supernatural marriage– Something in our voice activates the identification of our spouse. Your spiritual GPS and ID is in your voice! Our voice has been created for our spouse.

David and Jonathan were supernaturally connected via voice activation in 1 Sam 18:1. Jesus and John the Baptist were babies in the wombs of their mothers but again they recognised each other based on voice activation. Luke 1:39-45, In the stomach of their mothers, Elizabeth and Mary, the babies leaped, for joy!

1 Samuel 18:1 "*Now when he had finished speaking to Saul, the soul of Jonathan was knit to the soul of David, and Jonathan loved him as his own soul.*"

Luke 1:43-44 "*But why is this granted to me, that the mother of my Lord should come to me? For indeed, as soon as the voice of your greeting sounded in my ears, the babe leaped in my womb for joy.*"

A supernatural love will fill your heart when you meet your spouse. A supernatural release in the name of Jesus! Effortless love connection.

You'll be connected spiritually. The spirit of supernatural grace and love, shall knit your hearts together and connect you to each other. Incredible as it sounds, it is true.

Marital favour is bestowed on women before marriage to attract honour.

Because women are irresistible to men, and men are highly visual, and attracted by what they see, God desires women to be covered by His presence. Two factors determine the favour on women. Being covered by her earthy father and being covered by her heavenly father. Supernatural marriage is a transaction of honour. Without it, it does not work.

Without honour, the foundation for a healthy marriage relationship breaks down. Without honour, men are left to touch, taste, and gain access to women without making a commitment or paying a price. They receive rights and privileges that only those who have honoured the process should be receiving.

Ezekiel 16:8 *"When I passed by you again and looked upon you, indeed your time was the time of love; so I spread My wing over you and covered your nakedness. Yes, I swore an oath to you and entered into a covenant with you, and you became Mine," says the Lord God."*

The favour of God covers women. God the Father hates his daughters to be dishonoured and disrespected so He covers them with honour and favour. Even as the heavenly father covers His daughters spiritually and protects them from predators, counterfeits and unequal yokes, God is expecting earthly fathers to cover their daughters physically also. This sends a clear message to every potential suitor that she is a prize to be desired and attained by way of commitment to exclusivity, monogamy, love and lifelong sacrifice.

Dishonour due to being uncovered is one major factor why many single women, struggle to be married. If your Father was absent, or former boyfriends etc dishonoured you, it messes up the system of honour and invites others to try and continue the cycle. Be vigilant to cut off every opportunity to be dishonoured and stand your ground in the knowledge of your worth.

Dishonour is an evil spirit which works through people who want something for nothing OR they promise and fail. This is where broken engagements come from. People look good, say all the right things and before you know it, *for no reason*, they ghost and are gone!

Some make excuses as to why they promised but now can longer pursue the relationship. If you see this trend in your past relationships, you are fighting against a spirit of dishonour.

Dishonour also works against men, who are rejected or disrespected by family, friends and women too. They may invest, do everything correct yet they are treated as second class citizens. Their opinions are not regarded and their presence is not noted. David suffered this from his family. Joseph also. David was serving his family as a keeper of the sheep but his father and brothers did not as much as recognise him until Prophet Samuel asked, *"And Samuel said to Jesse, "Are all the young men here?" Then he said, 'there remains yet the youngest and there he is keeping the sheep."* **1 Samuel 16:11**. He came to anoint a king, and David was located from the wilderness because the Lord rejected the other sons of Jesse.. In Genesis 37, Joseph was sold into slavery by his own brothers due to envy and jealousy but again, their evil act was fuelled by the spirit of dishonour.

So my brothers, in you relationships, if you are complaining of women walking all over you, if they substitute you with another man, or marry you for what you have but not for who they are; know today, these are ALL manifestations of the spirit of dishonour.

Again Ancestral curses due to generational iniquity, in the blood line is another cause of dishonour. You will be able to identify it by being observant of the patterns you see running in your family.. Before you know it, the SAME thing which happened to your mother, grandmother or father and grandfather begin repeating themselves. By prayer, fasting and repenting you must break those evil cycles.

Sometimes you can spot the pattern by watching what has been going on with the marriages and relationships of the women in your family or men in your family. Best of all, in prayer, ask the Holy Spirit to reveal to you, where dishonour has taken its toll on you and those in your bloodline.

Once you identify generational or ancestral curses running in your bloodline, it is important you tackle it through the courts of heaven.

This book is not the place to fully break down the intricate details of why this needs to be done. However it is important for you to understand, the NATURE of God. His character is one of righteousness and justice which demands that all error is accounted for. There is a penalty in the kingdom of God for all transgression, sin and iniquity.

Exodus 34:5-7 *"Now the LORD descended in the cloud and stood with him there and proclaimed the name of the LORD. And the LORD passed before him and proclaimed, "The LORD, the LORD God, merciful and gracious, longsuffering, and abounding in goodness and truth,*

*Keeping mercy for thousands, forgiving iniquity and transgression and sin, **by no means clearing the guilty**, visiting the iniquity of the fathers upon the children and the children's children to the third and the fourth generation.""*

Moses had prayed and asked the LORD "show me your glory" to which He agreed to. So when the Lord revealed His glory, He revealed His nature, which is the perfection of His character.

The glory of God is holy character, and His character is just. The world did not invent justice, God did. True justice flows from His throne.

Psalm 89:14 *"Righteousness and justice are the foundation of Your throne; Mercy and truth go before Your face.*

God is merciful and releases mercy. But by no means can he clear the guilty. His system of justice would be broken. Somebody must pay. The word says the wages of sin is death.

Romans 6:23 *"For the **wages of sin is death**, but the gift of God is eternal life in Christ Jesus our Lord.*

The penalty is death, spiritual death; which impacts our quality of life, longevity of life and relationships on earth because it disconnects us from the eternal life of heaven.

Until we deal with the generational iniquity, sin and transgression in our personal lives and that committed by our ANCESTORS, the consequence continues. In the court of law, when a criminal is taken to trial, the penalty (judgement) is pronounced once. That is the same thing in the courts of heaven. For every 'crime' we commit against the word of God, either we pay of Christ pays. The penalty must be paid one way or another.

Isaiah 53:3-5 breaks it down like this:

"He is despised and [a]rejected by men,

A Man of [b]sorrows and acquainted with grief.

And we hid, as it were, our faces from Him;

He was despised, and we did not esteem Him.

Surely He has borne our griefs

And carried our [c]sorrows;

Yet we [d]esteemed Him stricken,

[e]Smitten by God, and afflicted.

But He was wounded for our transgressions,

He was [f]bruised for our iniquities;

The chastisement for our peace was upon Him,

And by His stripes we are healed."

So the Father, in His goodness found a way to be just. and still release us! Hallelujah. Through sending His own Son, Jesus to be crucified on the cross, He fulfilled divine justice and released us from the penalty.

We did the crime but He did the time! Lord we bless your holy name forever!

The Living God is a transgenerational He is described in scripture as the God of Abraham Isaac and Jacob (Exodus 3:6)

Genesis 12:3 *"in you shall the families of the earth be blessed.*

When the LORD blessed Abraham he was thinking about every person who would believe in Him for future generations." This also means, there are consequences generationally for our actions.

Just as the blessings are passed down so are the curses passed down. The good news is, you can break the cycle though faith in Christ. He paid with His own blood so you can be released and set free. Below we show you how to avail yourself to this option by faith and prayer.

Long story short, what our parents, grandparents and ancestry did to obey or rebel against the word of God affected us for good or bad. Many singles struggle to be married due to the presence of ancestral curse and this must be dealt and broken.

Until a sin or generational iniquity is REPENTED OF the consequence continues in that bloodline. When you see generational negative patterns happening in your life or you struggle to be free in an area, it is because of an OPEN DOOR. To break the stronghold, we have to remove the legal ground by closing the door.

Shut the Door and Be Delivered

The simple system we recommend is to use the pattern of prayer revealed in the book of Daniel chapter 9.

Study Daniel 9:1-19 who made confession for himself, fathers, kings, prophets, priests and nation. He was thorough! Be sensitive to the promptings of the Holy Spirit as you pray, Ask Him to reveal what areas need to be dealt with, and repent of each by name. Call it what He calls it. Very important. Making sin palatable is not the way to close the door, understand the Lord wants to release you but He is looking for sincere repentance first.

1. Confess and Repent
2. Renounce, Reject What Was Spoken and Done
3. Revoke all demonic agreements, covenants and oaths made to block marriage.
4. Ask the Lord to forgive and cleanse you by the Blood of Jesus (1 John 1:9)
5. You Are Exempted. And Released.

Restoring Divine Favour and Honour

Your mind must be renewed to be able to see yourself through the eyes of your Maker, which means you need saturate your soul in His Word.

Read Psalm 139,

Isaiah 62:1-4,

Songs of Solomon,

Isaiah 43:4,

John 15:9,

John 16:27.

These are just a few powerful esteem builders which express the value God places on you as His child. Men and Women who suffer from low self-worth need to work on this area. Remember you are not defined by what has happened to you. Your value is not defined by how others see you or treated you. It is easy to say, but hard to believe until your mind is renewed. When the Lord restores your identity and sense of value, He fortifies you against the spirit of dishonour and restores divine favour.

Men who have been dishonoured by parents or witnessed dishonour as the norm between their parents during their upbringing are prone to behaving dishonourably towards women in their life. Many find it difficult to either get married or stay married. They struggle to build right patterns of respectful communication. It is a spirit of dishonour. They begin to act out of the broken patterns they picked up from their past and unless they are mindful and intentional about breaking those patterns and establishing godly ones, there will be a problem.

Here are a few symptoms for you to judge if you are suffering from feelings of low self-worth: Insecurity, false bravado, boasting, pride (to cover deep sense of shame), a hard exterior, overly provocative and seductive dressing, smart mouth, posting obsessively on social media for likes, shares, comments, narcissism, controlling behaviour, abusive nature and possessiveness.

Low self-esteem, and insecurity in a person will either be internalised or projected negatively onto others but it always ends in dishonour. That's why it is so damaging. So allow the Lord to work this out of your system by building an intimate relationship with Him so He can show you, how valuable you are and equip you to withstand dishonourable advances. The danger of being insecure is, you will keep exposing yourself to people who want to use you or admire you, but never commit to you, simply because the attention makes you feel good for a while. When it is all over, they leave you more broken than when they came. It is not worth it!

Needless to say, establishing honour is crucial for us to get married and remain happily married. When it is the time of love, as a woman, it is imperative you do not present yourself to a man. Too many women buy into the lie that they have to uncover themselves with immodest dressing to present their 'goods' in order to win a man over. The devil is a liar.

Likewise men, stop chasing women, ask God for your wife, your rib, the bone of your bones, flesh of your flesh. The one created to be your help and favour. Supernatural Marriage is all about divine alignment in our relationships for the purposes of God and the glory of God. As much as love and attraction is involved, it holds a far deeper meaning than that. The price of obtaining a wife is the same prize Christ paid on the cross of calvary for his wife – LIFE. That is honour.

Divine favour is important in marriage but you need it even beyond marriage. Divine favour opens door in life and opens the hearts of people to bless you. Favour comes in levels and degrees. We grow in it like Jesus in Luke 2:52 and Prophet Samuel in 1:26. .

The LORD bestowed favour upon us during creation. (Psalm 8:5) Therefore if favour has been lost, and no man approaches you or no woman accepts you, add fasting and pray that the Lord restores divine favour over your life.

One last word on this. The difference between men and women is, women receive divine favour before marriage and men receive marital favour AFTER marriage.

When divine favour is bestowed upon a woman, this

facilitates her into marriage. Divine favour is bestowed upon men to prosper within marriage.

When God sees they have confirmed their commitment into a covenant and they position themselves as husbands, doors of favour are opened up to them on the earth. Many men are ignorant of this. Being single and righteous is a blessing but by divine design, there is a dimension of favour, single men do not walk in simply because Genesis 2:18, the Lord has already decreed, *'it is not good.'* Obviously this excludes men who are single by calling – like Apostle Paul, and Daniel.

For all other men, marital favour is released after marriage, to enable and empower him to fulfil one of the greatest roles and responsibilities any man can ever be given - becoming a godly husband. As a husband you are a leader, provider, protector, and father-figure to your family and society at large. Phew! That is why the Lord has added to you, the favour factor –your wife.

Proverbs 18:22 *"When a man finds a wife, he finds a good thing and receives favour from the Lord"*

STEP 6 – BE FRUITFUL, MULTIPLY & HAVE DOMINION

Prosper, Fulfil Divine Purposes, Bring God Glory.

Key scripture:

Genesis 1:28 *"Then God blessed them, and God said to them, "Be fruitful and multiply; fill the earth and subdue it; have dominion over the fish of the sea, over the birds of the air, and over every living thing that moves on the earth."*

In putting you into supernatural marriage, God is divinely positioning you to enjoy a replay of 'Eden'. Not a utopia, or paradise where nothing goes wrong. A spiritual place, which he delights in called Beulah – which means 'land of marriage'.

From the very beginning the Father desired mankind to walk with Him in this place called 'Eden'. So that we would learn of him, emulate him and showcase His Glory in our lives. The Word says, He blessed them (Adam and Eve) to propagate His divine model across the earth said 'be fruitful, multiply…fill the earth…. subdue it,…take dominion' In that order!

What do we have today?

People are fruitful

People are filling the earth,

People are subduing

People are taking dominion

Outside of the blessing parameters set by God. Instead of multiplying righteousness, peace

and joy over the earth, the world is busy multiplying wickedness, evil, chaos and confusion.

That is why God is intent on releasing singles and restoring kingdom couples into supernatural marriage in these last days. It is the platform upon which He will can build (rebuild) His original intention.

The Father never changed His mind.

He simply had to find a people who would renew theirs to agree with His.

Now you've received supernatural marriage, your focus is to prosper, which is to be **fruitful** and multiply in the kingdom of God, for the purposes of God, to the glory of God.

Just as each individual has a call, a purpose, or a reason for being, so does your marriage. Do not forget this.

Many marry and erroneously believe it is all about them. Men focus on getting their way with their wives and women focus on getting their way over their husbands. Others find a happy medium, but both forget about God's will. Their entire focus for marriage and life is on their will, their wishes, their plans and their family.

If that is you, you've missed the whole point.

Marriage is a foundation for family. A righteous family is the foundation for healthy society.
Therefore embedded in your marriage is the seed of influence, multiplication and dominion.
The enemy may resist your multiplication but now you know the way. Use the way of intercession, sacrifice, unity, service and diligence to multiply!

Maximise the power of agreement in your home. It is written one will chase a thousand, two will put ten thousand to flight.

God has positioned you in marriage in order to give you a spiritual advantage to multiply!

Remember your capacity to prosper is linked to your willingness to allow your soul (mind will and emotions) to prosper. (3 John 1:2)

The Way In teaches us, the way of Christ, in word, conduct, character and relationship. The more we apply 'the ways' of the Lord to our lives, the easier it will be for us to prosper. That is how the kingdom of God favours those who walk in His ways, it frustrates those who rebel against His ways. The world is the opposite. The world favours those who rebel and persecutes the righteous, but Jesus has overcome the world.

It boils down to, who will dominate. The people of God or the world. The world has it's methods and systems but we have the supernatural power of God on our side.

3 John 2 *"I wish above all things that thou mayest prosper, even as your soul does prosper"*

Psalm 1:1-3 *Blessed is the man who walks not in the counsel of the ungodly, nor stands in midst sinners, nor sits among the scornful, but his delight is the law of the Lord (his ways) and in it does He mediate day and night.....He shall be like a tree planted by the rivers of water.......**whatever he does shall prosper.***

Joshua was warned by the Lord, to meditate on the Word (Joshua 1:8), to be intentional about observing the ways of the Lord, then he would prosper. The root of prosperity is walking in the ways of the Lord. Living according to His principles. I have personally witnessed kingdom principles work to prosper people in the remotest villages of Africa to the most affluent cities of Europe, United Kingdom and America. Without discrimination.

This is the challenging part for most of us, because we want to do marriage our way. We want to maintain a good relationship with bad habits. We want to sustain our marriages without a heart of service or sacrifice. It won't work. It wasn't designed to work that way. The same way you received supernatural marriage is the same way you will have to sustain it. By being a doer of the Word, not a hearer only or preacher only.

This is where the rubber meets the road for millions of marriages. The choices we make can literally make or break our marriage.

We can blame the devil and make excuses for ourselves or we can learn the ways of the Lord.

All marriages have challenges, but God is committed to helping you overcome every challenge. For it to work, and for us to enjoy a happy marriage, we must be willing to walk in His ways. **That's the price. It is non-negotiable.**

Before we start jumping to Ephesians 5:22-33, let us first acquaint ourselves with **Ephesians 5:21** *"submitting to one another in the fear of God"*.... The foundation of submission and love in marriage is preceded with an instruction for us to walk in the fear of the Lord. This is our safety net. A healthy reverence and respect for God and each other is what the scriptures are talking about. Your marriage license does not license you, as a husband or wife to abuse the dignity, safety, purpose or esteem of your spouse.

Women Study Scriptures: *1 Peter 3:3-4, Luke 10:42, Luke 22:25-26, Ephesians 5:21-24*

Men Study Scriptures: *1 Peter 3:7-8, 1 Peter 5:3, Luke 22:25-26, Ephesians 5:25-33*

STEP 7 –GO SHOW OTHERS THE WAY

Now You've Attained it, Propagate It.

Key scripture:

Isaiah 62:4 *"You shall no longer be termed Forsaken, Nor shall your land any more be termed Desolate, But you shall be called Hephzibah, and your land Beulah;* **For the** L**ORD** **delights in you, And your land shall be married."**

Matthew 28:18-20 *"**Go therefore** and make disciples of all the nations, baptizing them in the name of the Father and of the Son and of the Holy Spirit, teaching them to observe all things that I have commanded you; and lo, I am with you always, even to the end of the age." Amen."*

Genesis 1:28 and Isaiah 62:4 are speaking of the same thing. God delighted to bless Adam and Eve because they fully represented His design to glorify Him on the earth.

Likewise the Lord will delight in you in your supernatural marriage. He is taking singles, broken marriages, divorcees, the solitary out of the status of feeling alone, single, forsaken and releasing them into a land, He has always delighted in – 'Beulah' meaning the land of marriage.

This is God's starting point for restoration. Men, women, marriage, family, church, society. This was His divine order in the beginning and this is the order the LORD is restoring now.

We wanted to build a great society, without great marriages. We wanted to build big churches on a house full of singles and failing marriages. We wanted to build strong families without strengthening their foundation; which is godly and peaceful unions. It is obvious from the

state of relationships around us, we have failed. Dysfunction seems to be on the increase. Not only in our relationships and homes but in the children whom we are raising. Sadly the divorce rate seems to be as high in the church as it is in the world. Because *'The Way In'* has not been taught or practiced. Christian believers have made a grave mistake by taking ideas from the world, tradition, or culture which are contrary to scripture, then we try to lay them down as the foundation for marriage in the church. God Jehovah, The Alpha and Omega is the initiator and originator of marriage and therefore He knows best how to save it. We must follow His Ways. Too many quoting the Word but resisting His ways.

Throughout scripture, God's best and highest will for life and marriage has always been, the supernatural way.

Jesus said it best when He simply stated to the religious leaders trying to ask him a trick question in Matthew 19:8 *"In the beginning, it was not so"*. Meaning, until you understand God's original plan in the beginning you will miss interpret the purpose of marriage. And we all know, whenever the purpose of a thing is misunderstood, abuse is inevitable.

He said, I am 'the way, the truth and the life' no man comes to the Father except by Me. (John 14:60. We limit this to salvation. Let us include marriage. The way of Christ is the way into marriage. Your conduct matters. Your character matters. Your ability to walk in humility, meekness and agape love matters. Your willingness to serve and sacrifice for your wife as a husband matters. Your submissive heart towards your husband matters. Both of you sustaining honour in preference of one another matters. Any other way WILL NEVER WORK in Christ. The devil is using our ignorance and stubbornness to his advantages. Before we bind him, talk to yourself. Change your ways. Submit to God, then resist the devil and the Word says, he will flee!

Any other way will not produce the effect of long lasting benefits God desires.

It is not about hooking up with a woman or man, it is about rightly aligning 'bone-to-bone' and 'flesh-to-flesh' according to divine purpose in the spirit of agape love.

Marriage to God is all about the covenant Christ made with us on earth. Through His shed blood on the cross, Jesus promised to *'never leave nor forsake us'* meaning I promise to be married to you and remain faithful to you forever.

May we be found faithful to walk worthy of this commitment. Not to deny Him or divorce him through our ways, disobedience, apostasy or idolatry.

The way of covenant is higher than commitment because covenant ties you in through a blood bond and sacrifice. It is sealed by oath or vows and lived out into eternity.

"Go and make disciples…" was the authoritative command of Jesus before He ascended into heaven. Go and show others. Go and teach others. Go and duplicate what you have received. Go and emphasize

MY WAY is superior than the ways of the world. Go!

Supernatural marriage: The Way In needs to be promoted because when you look at the issues of society, a majority of them are traceable back to issues in childhood, marriage or family breakdown. Simple. The devil hates marriage and will do anything to cause division and separation or singleness because he is fully aware of the damage he can cause in your life, destiny, children and society when this happens.

Any person who tells me they are serious about revival must in my view be committed to seeking the peace and release of godly marriages into the kingdom of God. Releasing singles into marriage has been renegaded in the Body of Christ to being to a lesser priority, than other

issues. Meanwhile I sense our Father in heaven bringing it centre forward as His priority.

In the beginning God begun with marriage between a man called Adam and his wife Eve (Genesis 2:22-25). The story of Israel and later the Church is based around the theme of marriage and in the end, (Revelation 19:7-8), we see the consummation of marriage between the Lamb and His wife. Marriage and every good thing that flows from it is central to the kingdom of God, not peripheral. It is time we placed it back where it belongs, at the top of our agenda.

Those who live for the Lord, in and through their marriage receive unending rewards and generational blessings into their lives.

I believe Abraham and Sarah best represented the picture of this while they were on earth. It is written of Abraham:

Genesis 24:1 *"Now Abraham was old, well advanced in age; and the* LORD *had blessed Abraham in all things"*

Then **in Galatians 3:29** we find out if we are Christ's then we are Abrahams seed and an heir according to the same promise He was given.

I truly believe, the 'all things' blessing is available only in Christ and Abraham gave us a pictorial view of what that looks like. I also believe one of the major reasons He received such an outpour of God's blessing was because He learned how to walk in the fear of the Lord with his wife Sarah, in love, transparency, honour and godly leadership all the days of his life. He was a living witness of the living God whom He served.

We are NOT meant to pursue all things but to walk in the fear of the Lord,.

We are meant to pursue His purposes and His Kingdom and Jesus promised us that 'all other things' will be added as necessary. (Matthew 6:33)

Everybody wants Abraham's blessings but how many are dedicated to The Way In – Supernatural Marriage?

Showing is telling. People can see how we live and behave and it will either encourage them to listen to what we are saying or influence them to reject it. You can't live like hell and speak of heaven. This is the litmus test too many believers, claiming Christ are failing. The responsibility to live like Christ in our marriages is even greater on Leaders. God sees us all in the secret place.

Abraham was called out of his family. He had to leave, and cleave to his wife, Sarah who was barren. No matter her shortcomings, their mistakes and failures, they stuck together, loved each other, and God fought for them and defended them in order to protect their union.

Why? Through their union and bloodline would come Christ.

He gave Abram a promise;

Genesis 12:3 *"I will bless those who bless you, And I will curse him who curses you; And in you all the families of the earth shall be blessed."*

Christ is the Grace, the Love, the Power and the Living Word through whom the World is blessed.

By exemplifying Christ in your marriage, you will become a blessing to your children, family and the families of the earth.

When husbands and wives both honour and love each other in marriage, we become an attractive signpost and advert for what God in Christ stands for: REAL LOVE

What the world needs now is REAL LOVE. So many people talk about it, sing about it, are in pursuit of love, but they don't know what love looks like? We think it is romance. We think it is sexiness, we think it is being admired, we think it is short lived, we think it is living only in pleasure, we think it is having everything we want whenever we want it, until we MEET Christ in person or see Him in others.

So, one of the greatest purposes of your marriage is to preach the gospel without saying a word!

Every supernatural marriage will tell a story of Christ. You relationship will showcase Him to the world in one way or another. To some, you will showcase unity, to others it will be seen through your hospitality. Others will showcase Christ as minsters, others healing, others creativity, wisdom, counsel or family. Your marriage will represent a visual aspect of His nature and character. Look out for it. Real Love is attractive when it is seen. I remember the Lord showing me, that in these last days, He will draw people from all walks of life to want to know Him based off what they see in the marriages of His people.

This is how the gospel will be preached to all the world. Not from pulpits alone, but from community platforms called supernatural marriages and kingdom families. Think about it. Families are in every community so wouldn't it be easier to get the word out organically through a system that exists everywhere!

God is reaching outside of the four walls of church auditoriums. He understands, thousands, if not millions of people may not necessarily go to a local church to find Christ, but He can easily connect them to a person and a family.

Jesus said this gospel will be preached to all the world, then the end will come. I am fully persuaded that the boat that Jesus will use in this modern era will be married couples and families sold out for Christ.

Matthew 24:14 "*And this **gospel** of the kingdom **will be preached** in all the world as a witness to all the nations, and then the end **will** come.*"

He repeated Himself before He ascended by saying

Acts 1:8 "*But you shall receive power when the Holy Spirit has come upon you; and you shall be witnesses to Me in Jerusalem, and in all Judea and Samaria, and to the end of the earth.*"

Your Jerusalem is your area of influence, your immediate family or locality. Jerusalem was the base for the disciples in those days, so Jesus was effectively saying, start where you are, with those in your local vicinity.

With these 7 proven keys, you have the blueprint on how to secure supernatural marriage as a man or woman in Christ.

With this information you literally have in your hands, the power to be married supernaturally – if only you will use it!

It is time for us to inherit our promised land of marriage called Beulah. It is time saints. Crossing over is our focus in this season. All the preparation, positioning, working, occupying means nothing if we do not SECURE supernatural marriage.

The certainty that you marriage awaits is based on the certainty that Jesus is coming back.

Never forget this. If Jesus is not lying about His return as our Bridegroom King, then neither is He lying about your release into supernatural marriage.

All that is left is for you is to make a decision. Are you willing to attain it? Are you willing to pay the price? God has already shown you His will in His word for your marriage but will you fight for it? When you look at the outcome, the fruits it will bear and the eternal impact it will make on your life, family and posterity, I think, you will agree; it is well worth it!

Take your time to document and journal your journey to supernatural marriage. This manual has been written to give you a simple road map into supernatural marriage with in-depth wisdom, revelation and encouragement to help you through the tough times.

I look forward to hearing your testimony. You will surely hear of mine.

Love and Prayers
Your supernatural marriage mentor
Evangelist Vivien Rose

PRAYERS AND DECLARATIONS

1. Lord, anything that's in me that's hindering me from my spouse, purge me of it in Jesus name.

2. Open they eyes of my husband to identify me (women)

3. Open the heart of my wife to receive me (men)

4. Knit our hearts together effortlessly O Lord (1 Samuel 18:1)

5. Deuteronomy 1:2-6 Pray against the spirit of delay! An 11 day's journey from Mt. Horeb took the children of Israel nearly 40 years and 11 months. That's the counsel of delay in operation!

6. Isaiah 54:17 – condemn every word that has risen against you and your marriage in the name of Jesus!!!!

7. Denounce Delayed Singleness! You name is Hephzibah and your land Beulah for the Lord delights in you and your land shall be married. (Isaiah 62:1)

8. Isaiah 8:9 – Be broken in pieces!! Shatter every plan of divination, sorcery ad witchcraft working against your marriage.

9. Psalm 35:1 May God contend against those who are contending against your promise of marriage.

10. Colossians 2:13-15 Repent of every sin and generational iniquity that has opened the door through your bloodline to hinder marriage. As you do this, reject and renounce every covenant, altar or agreement that was made to delay or stop your marriage.

11. Renew your covenant with the Lord through the Lord's supper and rededicate your life, and your marriage to God. The vow of dedication is what Hannah used to release the hand of God to work even before she received the blessing of a son. Hannah dedicated Samuel to God

before He was born. So dedicate your marriage to the purposes of God even before it manifests in your life.

Warning It is better not to vow than to vow and not to pay. Deuteronomy 23:21 "When you make a **vow** to the Lord your God, you shall not delay to **pay** it; for the Lord your God will surely require it of you, **and** it would be sin to you." Only do this when you are fully committed and sincere.

12. Deliver yourself from generational curse of singleness and marriage failure. Repent for yourself, and your family for every sin that has been committed against the word of God concerning marriage. For many, there is nobody who has sincerely confessed and repented of their family so the consequences are inherited until the blood of Jesus blots them out.

13. Ask the Lord to blot out the voice of sin, transgression and generational iniquity by the blood of Jesus.

14. Renounce every word, act, covenant, and declaration

made against marriage in your family and decree it shall not stand...Nullify it in the blood of Jesus!

15. Ask the Lord to restore the years the locusts have eaten in the area of marriage in your life and family.(Joel 2:25-26)

16. Come against the spirit of division, disagreement and discord that sows enmity into marriages. (Matthew 12:25)

17. Pray over your marriage and Abort the powers working to cause separation and divorce.

18. Pray against ungodly counsel from friends, family, loved ones, sent to delay, derail or deny you access to your ordained marriage. (Psalm 1:1-3)

19. Pray the Lord divinely connects you and accelerates the process of your engagement and marriage. (Ruth 3:18)

20. Pray and give God no rest until the matter of your marriage is settled (Isaiah 62:1)

21. Guard yourself and pray against the spirit of envy, jealousy and sabotage working to destroy your chances of marriage. (Job 5:12, Psalm 33:9-11)

22. Thank the Father for your wedding day according to Revelations 19:7-8.

23. Praise God for His faithfulness to perfect all things which concern you. (Psalm 138:8)

24. Pray to broke yokes of barrenness sent to delay your fruitfulness (Exodus 23:25-

25. Pray for God to bless the work of your hands and fruit of your labour, especially your future husband.(Isaiah 65:22-23)

26. Pray for divine provision and financial sufficiency over

your relationship and marriage. (2 Corinthians 9:8)

27. Declare we shall lack no good thing as we seek the Lord's will together (Psalm 34:10)

CONTACT

Apostle (Evg) Vivien Rose

Visionary of The Two Shall Be One

Website: www.thetwoshallbeone.com/getintouch

Email: thetwoshallbeone@gmail.com

YOUTUBE https://www.youtube.com/thetwoshallbeone

GIDEON WAR ROOM http://Bit.ly/Gideonarmyprayergroup

INSTAGRAM PAGES

For Singles https://www.instagram.com/thedayIgetmarried

FACEBOOK PAGES

For Singles https://www.facebook.com/thedayIgetmarried

For Marriage https://www.facebook.com/thetwoshallbeonepage

CONTACT

Website www.thewoshallbeone.com/getintouch

Subscribe to our email list

https://www.bit.ly/godlyrelationshiptipshere

Vivien Rose is a Visionary Founder and Apostolic Leader of The Two Shall Be One – an intercessory prayer & teaching ministry for singles and married couples dedicated to reviving the nations – one family at a time!

She carries an anointing for prayer, physical and emotional healing and deliverance. A Minister, Speaker and Author, Vivien Rose has served in ministry for almost 20 years. She is a prayer revivalist, intercessor and travels internationally for missionary work.

She has an incredible passion for marriage and gives powerful scriptural based teachings on relationships and marriage.

Vivien Rose is also an entrepreneur, talk show host and presenter. A devoted mother of two children, Vivien Rose is an impassioned advocate for survivors and sufferers of domestic violence and all forms of abuse.

Vivien Rose has written two books, "Winning The Battle Against Domestic Violence" a self-help guide for women seeking to get free from a controlling and abusive relationship and "Supernatural Husbands" - how to pray for your husband and husband-to-be. Both available on www.amazon.com and bookstore www.ignitepublishinghouse.com

A respected voice in the media, Vivien Rose is frequently interviewed on BBC Radio, BBC Television, Premier Christian Radio, Faith TV and various other media platforms. Vivien Rose travels regularly as conference speaker, and on missions to Africa and Asia, raising humanitarian aid and reaching out to the hurting and needy families in rural areas, towns and villages. **CONNECT:** TWITTER | FACEBOOK | INSTAGRAM **@Evg_VivienRo**

Printed in Great Britain
by Amazon